The Complete Crockery Cookbook

Create Spectacular Meals with Your Slow Cooker

by Wendy Louise

ISBN 1-891400-29-0
LCCN 2002111852

10 9 8 7 6 5 4 3

This book was printed in Canada.

For multiple sales or group discounts contact Champion Press, Ltd, 4308 Blueberry Road, Fredonia, WI 53021 – www.championpress.com

Contents

Dedication

This book is dedicated to the memory of Aunt Joan.
I would also like to thank Brook Noel for her fabulous
support and diligent editing. And to everyone at Champion
Press Ltd.—Thank you for making this book possible!

Introduction

Welcome to the world of slow-moist cooking. Like most good ideas, the concept of slow cooking has been around for a long, long time. Tried and true, it has simmered and braised meats to fork tender, root vegetables to perfection and even desserts to savory sweetness.

From the Marmite Pot to the Bean Pot, the Chinese Clay Pot to the Colonial Dutch Oven, succulent meals have been slowly cooked for centuries. –Perhaps the first 'slow cooker' was fashioned from an earthen pit lined with heated rocks, or smoldering embers, piled high with wild game and gathered vegetables wrapped in moistened corn husks or huge banana leaves. Covered over with a mound of earth the food cooked, unattended, while people went about their daily tasks of survival. With the advent of the electric slow cooker in the 1970's, slow cooking was raised to a "modern art form". Based on ancient concepts (i.e. good food, easily prepared), the slow cooker brought economy, convenience and flexibility to the modern-day kitchen.

But that was 1970 and this is the 21st Century you say…Well, just think about it for a minute…Wouldn't it be nice to by-pass a stop at the Deli, the Drive-In, the Take-out…and come directly home (your time and budget intact) to a wonderful meal, completed to perfection in your very own kitchen? Just imagine the 'instant gratification' of returning after a long day at work or school, opening the door and taking in those first, comforting aromas of your awaiting meal. With a little advanced planning and prep work in the morning, your family can sit down to an economical and nutritious meal in the evening. And won't **you** enjoy it more...knowing 'clean up' is a breeze, when the meal is over!

With the mastery of a few basic concepts and a little creativity, you too can enjoy the benefits of slow cooking. This book is meant to provide you with just such ideas and to entice you into the delicious world of family-style, slowly-cooked crockery-meals.

"Getting Started..."

Slow cookers come in a variety of sizes —from one-quart capacity for singles and small recipes, to six-quart capacities for six persons plus and larger style cooking. To take full advantage of your slow cooker, the recipe should fill the pot at least half-full to three-quarters full for maximum cooking performance. You may find you will want to have more than one slow cooker (perhaps in varying sizes) to enhance your cooking capacity...a small one for that dip you are serving at a party, a large one for that whole chicken, soup or stew and even a medium size for a side dish or dessert.

Most commonly slow cookers have two settings: the "Low" setting which cooks at approximately 200 degrees F. and the "High" setting which cooks at approximately 300 degrees F. The Low setting is great for all-day and unattended cooking; allowing for flexibility of timing and 'holding' food (with little worry about drying-out or scorching your meal) —a perfect solution when you are caught in that traffic-commute after work or the boss has had you stay late to meet a day-end-deadline. The High setting is great for Saturday and Sunday meals, when you might want to cut your cooking time in half. Throw in a couple loads of laundry or craft in your scrap book; go to a movie or sit down and watch the football game; play baseball with the kids or go to the gym; take a quick shopping trip to the mall or put your feet up and read a good book. Before you know it your meal is done and you have been far a field from the kitchen! The general rule is 1 hour of slow cooking on High is equal to about 2-2 1/2 hours of slow cooking on Low...Or in layman's terms, 1 hour of cooking time (out of the kitchen) spent at the gym is equal to 2-2 1/2 hours of cooking time spent (out of the kitchen) watching a good movie... 'Sounds good to me!...how about you?

There are a few basic safety rules that should be meticulously followed when using your slow cooker. After cooking and serving your meal, the remaining food should **not** be stored in or reheated in the slow cooker. Foods that are left to cool to below 185 degrees F for any extended period of time are greatly susceptible to the growth of bacteria. So promptly transfer your leftovers to a container for the fridge and do your reheating in a microwave, on the stove or in the oven. If you are assembling your dish the night before (and storing it in the refrigerator) **do not** mix-in any raw meats. Add them in the morning just before you start the cooking process. (Any raw marinades should be discarded if not incorporated directly into the cooking process.)

Slow cookers are designed for just that, slow and gentle cooking. To avoid cracking, do not subject your crockery liner to extreme and abrupt changes of heat. If you have assembled your dish the night before and are transferring it from the fridge to the heating coils do not attempt to 'pre-heat' the base unit to speed up the process, so to speak. Put the chilled and filled liner into the base unit and turn it on Low. It will warm up gently and simmer all day.

Likewise, when cleaning your crockery insert make sure to treat it with the same gentle respect, avoiding abrupt temperature changes. Avoid using abrasive cleaners, as they may scratch the glazed surface of the liner. Spraying your liner with cooking spray before assembling and cooking your dish also makes for quick and easy cleanup. (And, obviously, do not submerge the electrical portion in water.)

It sounds mundane, but don't forget to turn-off and unplug your slow cooker when done! A good 'rule of thumb' is to get in the habit of "turning off and unplugging" **before** you remove your finished dish to the table. Many a story has been told about removing the liner and leaving the base unit heating away on the counter! These basics said, be sure to look for more "tips, tricks and info" interspersed within the text of this book. You'll find Cook's Notes, offering serving suggestions and great variety. And *TIPS FROM THE KITCHEN* offer a multitude of information and ideas to guide you along. The recipes for this book have been selected to offer a wide range of versatility from simple to formal and to please all palates. So let's plug in the pot and get cookin'...

Chapter One:
Soup's On

Soups, Stews, Chilies and Beans

"Soup's on..." Serve up a soup, stew or chili from this chapter and you won't have to yell "soup's on..." very loud to get their attention. You will also find some great bean dishes to add to your menus.

Soup's On Chapter Index

Apple Barley Soup

20 servings

7 large onions, thinly sliced
7 tablespoons vegetable oil
12 cups vegetable stock
5 cups apple cider
1-2 cups pearl barley
7 large carrots, diced
4 teaspoons thyme
5 teaspoons dried marjoram
3 bay leaves
5-6 teaspoons McCormick's Season-All®
7 cups unpeeled-chopped apples
1 scant cup fresh parsley
3-4 tablespoons lemon juice

Sauté the sliced onions over medium-high heat until softened and brown. Transfer to slow cooker. Add stock, cider, barley, carrots, thyme, marjoram, bay leaves and Season-All®. Cover with lid and cook on high for 3-4 hours, or until barley is almost tender. Add apples, parsley and lemon juice. Cover and continue to cook on high setting until apples and barley are tender, but not mushy, approximately 1 more hour. Do not raise up lid as you will lengthen cooking time by letting out built-up temperature and steam. Discard bay leaves before serving.

-from the kitchen of Kathy Gulan

Kathy's Asparagus Potato Soup

20 servings

3 ½ pounds asparagus, trimmed and cut into 1-inch
  lengths
3-4 large potatoes, peeled and cut into 1/2 -inch cubes
3-4 medium yellow onions, peeled and cut into slim wedges
12 cups chicken broth
3/4 teaspoon ground mace
1/2 teaspoon ground nutmeg
1-2 teaspoons salt, or to taste
1 teaspoon freshly ground pepper
7 shakes McCormick's Season-All®
20 tablespoons freshly grated Parmesan cheese

Place all ingredients, accept Parmesan cheese, in a large
slow cooker. Cover with lid and cook on low setting all day,
or until vegetables are very tender. Cool the soup, still
covered, for 20 minutes or so. Puree the soup, in batches, in
a blender or food processor fitted with a metal chopping
blade. Ladle into heated soup bowls and top each serving
with a sprinkling of 1 tablespoon Parmesan cheese.

—*from the kitchen of Kathy Gulan*

A Tip from the Kitchen...
When garnishing with Parmesan cheese freshly grated
makes all the difference in the world! Parmesan curls are
nice too. Use your potato peeler to shave off curls from the
wedge of cheese directly onto the soup.

Penny's Black Bean Soup

8 servings

1 pound dried black beans
Water (to cover beans)
2 teaspoons baking soda
1 smoked ham-hock
6 cups water
3 beef bouillon cubes
1 tablespoon olive oil
2 green bell peppers, finely chopped
2 large onions, finely chopped
1 clove garlic, finely chopped
1 teaspoon ground cumin
1 can diced tomatoes with juice
1/4 cup red wine vinegar
1 tablespoon minced fresh coriander
Sour cream for garnish

Wash dried beans and put them in a large soup pot. Cover with water and bring to a hard boil on the stove top. Boil beans for about 5 minutes then transfer pan to sink. Drop in 2 teaspoons of baking soda. This will make the beans foam. Stir well and drain in colander. Rinse beans in cold water 2 times. (Your beans are now ready to be used in your recipe.) Put rinsed beans in the slow cooker. Add ham-hock, water, beef bouillon cubes, olive oil

and cumin. Cover with lid and cook on high setting for 6 hours. In a blender, combine chopped green pepper, chopped onion, minced garlic, diced tomatoes, red wine vinegar and fresh coriander. Puree the contents and add to the slow cooker. Stir to blend well. Reduce heat to low setting, cover with lid and continue cooking for an additional 4 hours. Serve with a dollop of sour cream as a garnish.

Excerpted from Crazy about Crockery! 101 Soups and Stews ISBN 1891400126 by Penny E. Stone

A Tip from the Kitchen...
Pureeing a portion or all of your soup makes for a thicker, smoother, silkier soup.

Cream of Carrot Soup
6-8 servings

8-10 medium to large carrots, sliced, then grated

1-2 cups diced celery

3 medium to large white potatoes, peeled and diced

6 cups canned chicken broth

1 teaspoon salt

1 pint heavy cream

Salt and white pepper to taste

Dash of nutmeg

Finely grate all the carrots. Reserve 1 cup grated carrot, but put the remainder in slow cooker. Combine diced celery, diced potatoes, chicken broth and 1 teaspoon salt in slow cooker. Cover with lid and cook on high setting for 4-6 hours. Turn heat off and let contents cool. Transfer 2 cups of vegetables with broth to blender and puree, return mixture to slow cooker. Continue until all vegetables have been pureed. Add heavy cream and adjust seasonings according to taste with salt and pepper. Add the reserved grated carrot. Cover with lid, reduce heat to low setting, and continue cooking for 2-3 hours. Serve in warmed soup bowls with a sprinkling of nutmeg over each serving.

Excerpted from Crazy About Crockery! 101 Soups and Stews ISBN 1891400126 by Penny E. Stone

A Tip from the Kitchen...
Dairy products such as milk, cream, sour cream, cream cheese and cheeses can curdle and separate if cooked for too long or at too high a temperature. Try to add these during the last hour of cooking or incorporate them on low setting when possible.

Cream of Celery Soup

6 servings

4 cups chopped celery stalks (Use the inner stalks of the
lighter colored celery for best results. These are also
known as celery hearts and can be bought as such in your
produce market.)
1 large onion, chopped
6 cups chicken broth
2 cups half-and-half cream or heavy cream
3 tablespoons butter or margarine
2 tablespoons cornstarch, dissolved in 1/2 cup cool water or
white wine , with salt and white pepper to taste

In your slow cooker combine 3 cups of the chopped celery
with half of the chopped onion and all of the chicken broth.
Cover with lid and cook on high setting for 6-7 hours. Then,
in a skillet melt the butter and sauté remaining chopped
onion and remaining cup of chopped celery until the
vegetables are tender. Add to the skillet the
cornstarch/wine or water mixture and the 2 cups of cream.
Simmer over medium heat, stirring constantly, until
mixture begins to thicken and just comes to a boil.
Meanwhile remove contents from slow cooker and puree in
batches in a blender. Return pureed mixture to slow cooker.
Add the skillet-cream mixture to slow cooker and blend
both until incorporated. Adjust salt and white pepper to
taste, being careful not to over season. Cover with lid and
reduce to low setting, continue to cook for 2-3 more hours,
allowing all flavors to blend into a delicate creamy soup.

*Excerpted from Crazy About Crockery! 101 Soups and Stews ISBN
1891400126 by Penny E. Stone*

Crock-potato Cheese Soup

6 servings

2 pounds potatoes, peeled and cubed
1 onion, chopped
5 cups chicken broth or vegetable broth
Salt and pepper to taste
1 cup milk, 1 % low-fat, or use soy milk
1 cup Cheddar cheese, low-fat, shredded

Cook the first three ingredients, along with the salt and pepper, in a covered slow cooker for 3 hours on high setting, or until potatoes are done and tender. Process half the potato mixture in a food processor; pour back into pot, stirring well to thicken the soup. Turn slow cooker to low setting. Add the milk stirring well to incorporate. Continue to simmer on low heat. (You do not want to boil the soup, or the milk will separate.) Correct the seasoning, to your taste, with additional salt and pepper. To serve, ladle up generous portions and top each bowl with shredded Cheddar cheese.

Excerpted from Healthy Foods, an irreverent guide to understanding nutrition and feeding your family well ISBN 1891400207 by Leanne Ely, C.N.C.

A Tip from the Kitchen...

"Guild the lily"...When possible garnish your slow-cooked dishes with a fresh ingredient. Chopped fresh parsley, fresh chives from the garden, diced sun-dried tomatoes, homemade croutons, a little grated lemon zest, crisped bacon bits, freshly grated cheeses or cheese curls...the contrast of texture will add surprise and interest to your meal and an extra touch that makes it special.

Curried Lentil Soup

6 servings

Cook's Note: "A perfectly delicious soup for a cold, winter day..."

2 teaspoons olive oil
1 cup chopped onion
1 ¼ teaspoons curry powder
3 cups water
4 cups chicken broth
3 cups lentils (or use one package amount)
2 teaspoons basil
2 tablespoons balsamic vinegar
1 (14.5 ounce) can diced tomatoes, un-drained
Salt and pepper to taste

Heat oil in large Dutch oven over medium-high heat. Add onion and sauté for about 4 minutes. Add curry and sauté another minute. Add water, chicken broth and lentils, and bring to a boil. Transfer to slow cooker. Cover with lid and cook on high setting 3-4 hours, or on low setting 7-8 hours, until lentils are tender. Place about half of the lentil-soup-mixture into a blender and process until smooth. Return to the slow cooker and mix well to incorporate. Add basil, balsamic vinegar, salt and pepper to taste, and the tomatoes. Continue to cook until thoroughly heated.

Excerpted and adapted from The Frantic Family Cookbook (mostly) healthy meals in minutes ISBN 1189400118 by Leanne Ely, C.N.C.

Creamy Tomato Soup with Cognac

6-8 servings

15-16 garden tomatoes, scalded and slipped out of their
  skins, but left whole
1 onion, chopped
3 tablespoons butter
1 teaspoon sweet basil, crushed between fingers
1 pint heavy cream
1 teaspoon brown sugar
Salt and white pepper
4-5 tablespoons cognac, or to
  taste
1 tablespoon butter

Sauté the chopped onion quickly
in a little butter and transfer to
slow cooker. Semi-smash the
scalded and skinned tomatoes
with a fork and add to slow
cooker. Add the sweet basil.
Cover with lid and simmer on low setting for 5-7 hours, or
until all is stewed and juicy. Force the tomato mixture
through a sieve and discard the pulp and seeds. Put the
smoothed mixture back into the slow cooker. Heat the
heavy cream with the teaspoon of brown sugar (but do not
boil) and stir into the tomato-base, whisking all the while.
Do not allow soup to boil. Season with salt and white
pepper to taste. In a ladle, flame 4-5 tablespoons of cognac

and fold into soup. Swirl in 1 tablespoon of butter to 'finish' the soup. Serve warm as a first course.

-from the kitchen of Juan Alduncin, as enjoyed on the Island of Cozumel

A Tip from the Kitchen...

To easily remove the skins from fresh tomatoes drop the tomatoes into scalding water for 30 seconds, remove with slotted spoon and plunge into ice water. The skins will peel off easily. **Kitchen Side Note:** This scalding method works equally well for skinning peaches.

Lentil and Rice Soup

10 servings

1 (12 ounce) can tomato paste
2 (16 ounce) cans tomatoes with juice
8 cups water
2 cups uncooked lentils
2 cups uncooked long grain rice
2 medium onions, chopped
2 cloves garlic, minced
Salt and pepper to taste

Put canned tomatoes (and their juice) and the tomato paste in slow cooker. Add water and stir well. Stir in all other ingredients. Salt and pepper to taste. Cover with lid and simmer on low for 8-10 hours (or high for 4-6 hours) until lentils are soft and rice is cooked. Adjust seasonings if necessary.

Excerpted and adapted from Frozen Assets, cook for a day and eat for a month by Deborah Taylor-Hough ISBN 1891400614

A Tip from the Kitchen...

of Deborah Taylor-Hough ... When chopping onions, Deborah recommends chopping more than you need for your recipe. Package in portioned sizes in freezer bags and store in freezer (for up to 2 months) for future recipes. Next time your recipe calls for chopped onion it will be ready and waiting...no muss, no fuss.

London Fog Split Pea Soup

8 servings

2 cups split peas, rinsed and picked over
2 tablespoons olive oil
1 onion, chopped
2 carrots, diced
10 cups of water
1 ham hock (or one smoked turkey leg)
1 teaspoon thyme
Salt and pepper to taste

Put the cleaned split peas in a slow cooker. In a skillet, heat the oil over medium heat. Sauté the onion and carrots for about 3 minutes and then transfer to slow cooker. Fill the slow cooker with 10 cups of water and bury the ham hock (or smoked turkey leg) into the peas. Add the thyme, along with salt and pepper to taste. Cover with lid and cook on low setting for 8-10 hours. Remove ham hock (or turkey leg) from slow cooker, shred or dice the meat from the bone and return to soup.

Cook's Note: Serve with crusty bread and a big salad.

Excerpted and adapted from The Frantic Family Cookbook (mostly) healthy meals in minutes ISBN 1189400118 by Leanne Ely, C.N.C.

A Tip from the Kitchen...
Soups make a satisfying yet light dinner when accompanied with crusty French bread and a salad. Splurge with a fantastic dessert, after this simpler meal, and you will be well satisfied.(Check out the dessert section on pages 210 - 230.)

Split Pea Soup with Ham

8 servings

10 cups water, chicken broth, or mixture of both
4 cups dry split peas
1 cup diced ham
1 teaspoon salt
1/2 teaspoon pepper
1/4 teaspoon crushed, marjoram
1 bay leaf
1 cup chopped celery
1 cup chopped onion
1 cup sliced carrots

Wash and sort dried peas, removing any stones. Place all ingredients in slow cooker. Cover with lid and simmer on low heat for 8-10 hours (or on high for 6 hours) until peas are tender.

Excerpted and adapted from Frozen Assets, cook for a day and eat for a month by Deborah Taylor-Hough ISBN 1891400614

A Tip from the Kitchen...

What goes better with soup than crackers...it's an automatic! Don't forget those old fashioned oyster crackers! As a child I remember plopping those little puffy crackers into my soup. Toss them with a little melted butter and some seasonings, crisp in a 350-degree oven for about 10 minutes and you have an excellent garnish for your slowly cooked soup. The oyster crackers may also be crisped, uncovered, using the high setting of your slow cooker; or they may be stirred up in a pan. Once cooled, store in an airtight container and use as a snack or garnish.

Cook's Side Note: Your favorite Party Mix can be made in the same fashion, in the slow cooker, as opposed to the oven. Combine your assorted cereals, nuts, crackers and pretzels, along with melted butter and your seasonings of choice and 'toast' in uncovered slow cooker. Use high setting for 1 hour and then reduce to low setting for 2-4 hours more, stirring every so often. Serve warm straight from the pot! Store cooled in airtight container.

A Tip from the Kitchen...

For an elegant touch try seasoning with white pepper in light colored soups and sauces. Save the black pepper for stews, chilies and brown sauces.

Aunt Joan's German Bean Soup

6-8 servings

2 1/2 cups dry kidney beans, soaked overnight and drained

6 slices bacon, finely chopped, sautéed and drained

1 cup diced onion

1 cup diced carrots

2 cups diced celery

2 cups diced potatoes

1/2 cup canned tomato puree

2 bay leaves

2 cloves garlic, smashed and minced

1 tablespoon salt

1/4 teaspoon pepper

6 cups cold water

4 cups canned beef broth

2 tablespoons red wine vinegar

2 cups sliced garlic sausage (fully cooked)

1 cup thinly sliced leeks (or sliced green onions, including tops)

Place all ingredients (except last 3) in slow cooker. Cover with lid and simmer on low setting 8-10 hours, until beans are tender and flavors have melded. Puree half of the soup mixture in blender, being careful to remove the bay leaves. Return all to slow cooker and add the vinegar, garlic sausage and thinly sliced leek (or green onion). Continue to heat until all is warmed. (Leek or onion will be tender-crisp.) Serve as a hearty main course with crusty French bread.

Cook's Note: For a different taste and texture, substitute Great Northern beans for the kidney beans in this recipe.

-from the kitchen of Joan Sennett

Snappy Black Bean Soup

12 servings

2 cups black beans, rinsed
  and soaked overnight
2 tablespoons olive oil
1 onion, chopped
2 cloves garlic, pressed
2 teaspoons cumin

2 cups chicken broth
1 cup jarred salsa
Sour cream, for garnish
  (optional)
Minced green onion, for
  garnish (optional)

In a slow cooker, place your soaked beans. In a skillet, heat oil and sauté onion and garlic together for 3 minutes, or until onion is soft. Add this mixture to the slow cooker. Then add cumin, and chicken broth. Cover with lid and cook on low setting all day—about 8 hours. Stir in the salsa just before serving.

Cook's Note: You can serve this soup topped with sour cream and green onions, if you like.

Excerpted and adapted from The Frantic Family Cookbook (mostly) healthy meals in minutes ISBN 1189400118 by Leanne Ely, C.N.C.

A Tip from the Kitchen...

With the exception of lentils and split peas, dried beans should always be 'soaked' before using in a slow cooker. A simple method is to parboil them, covered with water, for 2-3 minutes. Let them stand for at least an hour. Then drain and rinse them and add to the pot; or set aside until needed. A convenient alternative is to use drained and rinsed canned beans if you prefer. ***Kitchen Side Note:*** Penny Stone presents another soaking method, explained on page 14, in her Black Bean Soup recipe.

Mike's Bean, Ham Bone and White Corn Soup

10-12 servings

1 (16 ounce) package Great Northern white beans
1 ham bone, with a little meat on
1 (15.25 ounce) can whole kernel white corn, un-drained
2 (14.5 ounce) cans chicken stock
Additional water if needed
1 tablespoon dried, crushed oregano
1/2 teaspoons paprika
1/2 teaspoon chili powder
1/2 teaspoon Season-All® type seasoning
1-3 bay leaves
1 large onion, chopped
3 stalks celery, chopped
3 carrots, diced
2 garlic cloves, smashed and minced
1 jalapeno pepper, seeded and quartered
2 (14.5 ounce) cans stewed or diced tomatoes, pureed
Sliced green onions to taste, including tops
Cayenne (optional)
Red Pepper Flakes (optional)

Soak the beans overnight in water to cover. Remove meat from hambone and cut into 1/2 –inch cubes, to about 3 cups. Set aside.

Drain the beans and place in slow cooker, along with the carved hambone. Add corn, chicken stock, additional water if needed to cover, and the seasonings. Cover with lid and cook on high setting for 3-4 hours.

Add the remaining ingredients, except for the reserved ham cubes and the green onions, and mix well. Reduce heat to low setting, cover with lid and continue to cook for about 5 more hours. If you like, during this second-cooking segment you can add cayenne and red pepper flakes to add even more flavor. About 30 minutes from end of cooking time remove bay leaves; mash some of the beans against the side of the liner to thicken the soup slightly; add the reserved ham cubes and the sliced green onions. Adjust seasonings if necessary.

Cook's Note: The soup can be served as a complete meal by itself or over rice for an added treat.

Recipe contribution by Michael Gulan, Champion Press Ltd. Publishing Assistant

Chicken Corn Chowder

8 servings

2 tablespoons butter or margarine

An all-purpose seasoning to taste

1 ½ pounds chicken tenders, cut into 1/2 -inch cubes

2 small onions, chopped

2 celery ribs, sliced

2 small carrots, sliced

2 cups frozen sweet corn, thawed

2 cans cream of potato soup

1 ½ cups chicken broth

1 teaspoon dried dill weed

1/2 -1 cup half-and-half cream

Salt and white pepper to taste

In a large skillet melt the butter and sprinkle in an all-purpose seasoning to taste. Add the cubed chicken and sauté till lightly browned. Transfer the chicken to the slow cooker. Add the next seven ingredients to the slow cooker, cover with lid and cook on low setting 5-6 hours, or until chicken is done and veggies are tender. During the last 15 minutes of cooking add the half-and-half cream and adjust the seasoning to taste with salt and white pepper.

Recipe contribution by Michael Gulan, Champion Press Ltd. Publishing Assistant

A Tip from the Kitchen...

A pat of butter swirled into a soup, sauce or stew at the very last minute adds depth and hidden flavor to the dish. It's just one little pat! French cooks have used this secret for years...by 'finishing' their sauce with a little swirl of butter. Used sparingly, it's a nice addition to your repertoire.

Corny Chicken and Potato Chowder

4 servings

1 tablespoon olive oil
6 slices turkey bacon, chopped (optional)
2 medium onions, chopped
2 cans chicken broth
2 good sized potatoes, peeled and cut into 1/2 -inch pieces
4 cups corn kernels, frozen or canned
2 cups cooked chicken, chopped
1 ½ teaspoons thyme
1 cup milk
Salt and pepper to taste

Cook bacon with olive oil in a large saucepan over medium-high heat until brown and crisp (about 5 minutes). Remove bacon to paper towels and drain, setting aside for later. Add onion, sautéing until soft (about 3 minutes). Place soft onions in slow cooker. Add broth to the skillet. Turn up heat and with a wire whisk get up all the browned bits from the bottom of the saucepan. Pour the broth into the slow cooker and add the potatoes. Cover and let cook on low setting for 8 hours. Turn slow cooker to high setting and add corn, chicken, thyme and milk. Cover with lid and allow to cook for another hour. Season the chowder to taste with salt and pepper. Ladle into bowls. Crumble bacon over the top and serve.

Excerpted and adapted from The Frantic Family Cookbook (mostly) healthy meals in minutes ISBN 1189400118 by Leanne Ely, C.N.C.

The Rush Hour Cook's Chicken Dumpling Soup

Served with Old Fashioned Dumplings

6 servings

1 ½ pounds chicken (white meat), cut into pieces
4 (14.5 ounce) cans chicken broth
4 corresponding cans of water
1 large onion, chopped
4 carrots, chopped
2 celery stalks, chopped
1 teaspoon salt
1 teaspoon garlic powder
1/2 teaspoon pepper
1/2 teaspoon chicken bouillon granules

Brown chicken pieces in a non-stick skillet and transfer to slow cooker. Add the chopped vegetables, broth, water and seasonings. Cover with lid and cook on low setting 6-8 hours, until chicken is done and vegetables are tender. Add dumplings (see recipe next page) to soup. Cover with lid and turn heat setting to high; continue cooking for another half hour, or until dumplings are shiny and set.

Old Fashioned Dumplings

1/2 cup cottage cheese
2 tablespoons water
1/2 teaspoon salt
1 cup flour
3 egg whites

Beat egg whites and cottage cheese thoroughly. Blend in the salt and water. Stir in the flour, a bit at a time, mixing well, until all is incorporated. Drop dumpling mixture by tablespoonfuls into the simmering soup. Cover with lid and cook until dumplings are set.

Cook's Note: (If you prefer) the dumplings may be cooked in a large pot of boiling-salted water for approximately 15 minutes and then added to the soup in the slow cooker.

Excerpted and adapted from The Rush Hour Cook presents Family Favorites ISBN 1891400835 by Brook Noel

Hamburger Soup

6 servings

2 pounds lean ground beef, browned and drained
2 teaspoons dried basil
2 teaspoons crushed oregano
2 teaspoons garlic powder
5-6 cups tomato juice
1 cup stewed tomatoes
1 large onion, chopped
2 cups chopped celery
1 cup sliced carrots
2 cups sliced green beans
1 tablespoon Worcestershire sauce
Salt and pepper to taste

Place browned meat in slow cooker. Add all remaining ingredients and stir to mix well. Cover with lid and simmer on low setting for at least 5 hours. Serve steaming hot, with old fashioned oyster crackers on the side. (See Tip from the Kitchen, page 24.)

Excerpted and adapted from 365 Quick, Easy and Inexpensive Dinner Menus ISBN 1891400339 by Penny E. Stone

Country Beef Soup

6 servings

6 cups water
3 cups canned Italian-style
  stewed tomatoes,
  chopped (and their juice
  reserved for the soup)
1 pound potatoes, washed
  peeled and 1/2-inch cubed
1 pound cooked beef, diced
1 1/2 cups sliced celery
1 1/2 cups sliced

mushrooms
1 1/2 cups sliced carrots
1 cup chopped onion
1 cup frozen whole kernel
  corn
6 packets instant beef
  broth/seasoning mix
2 tablespoons chopped
  parsley
1 teaspoon pepper

Combine all ingredients in slow cooker. Cover with lid and simmer on low setting all day.

Cook's Note: "On the way home from work, pick up a loaf of freshly baked French bread from your grocery store bakery department. Crisp and warm in oven. Break off chunks of bread (European style) and slather with unsalted butter. Serve along side steaming bowls of soup for a rustic, country dinner."

Excerpted from Frozen Assets Lite and Easy, cook for a day and eat for a month by Deborah Taylor-Hough ISBN 1 891400282

A Tip from the Kitchen...
There is nothing better on warm French bread than unsalted butter! Unsalted butter has a dynamic all its own. Use the whipped variety and you will use less butter and, thusly, consume less calories per slice of 'slathered' bread.

Not-a-Soup, Not-a-Stew Chicken

6 servings

2 pounds boneless chicken breasts, cut into bite-sized
   pieces
1 onion, chopped
1 cup chopped celery
4 cloves garlic, minced
3 cans chicken broth
1 cup water
1 ½ cups frozen mixed vegetables (broccoli, cauliflower,
   and bean combination), thawed
1 ½ cups frozen peas, thawed
1 ½ cups frozen carrots, thawed
1 (8 ounce) package of egg noodles, partially cooked
1 teaspoon salt
1/4 teaspoon
   pepper

In a skillet, lightly
brown the chicken
pieces, along with
the onion and
garlic, in a little
olive oil, about 5-8
minutes. Toss in
the celery and cook
for another 1-2
minutes over medium heat. Transfer to a slow cooker and
add remaining vegetables (except peas), chicken broth,

water, salt and pepper. Cover with lid and cook on high setting for 4-6 hours, or low setting 8-10 hours. Last hour of cooking, add the partially cooked egg noodles and finally the peas, cooking until the noodles are tender, and peas are cooked but not mushy. Adjust seasonings of salt and pepper to your taste.

Cook's Note: Serve with French bread for a complete meal.

Excerpted and adapted from The Rush Hour Cook presents Effortless Entertaining ISBN 189140086X by Brook Noel

A Tip from the Kitchen...
When adding noodles to your slowly cooked soup, partially cook them before-hand to avoid sticky noodles and starchy soup.

Mama's Chicken Stew

10 servings

1 pound skinned, boneless chicken breasts, cut into bite-size pieces
1 pound skinned, boneless chicken thighs, cut into bite-size pieces
1/2 cup water
1 cup frozen small onions
1/2 cup celery, sliced
1 cup carrots, sliced thin
1 teaspoon paprika
1/2 teaspoon sage
1/2 teaspoon thyme
2 teaspoons garlic powder
Salt and pepper to taste
2 (14.5 ounce) cans chicken broth
1 (6 ounce) can tomato paste
2 cups frozen petite green peas
1/4 cup water
3 tablespoons cornstarch

Combine chicken pieces with all ingredients (except the last three listed) and place in slow cooker. Cover with lid and cook on high setting for 4 hours, or until chicken pieces are done and carrots are fork tender. Combine the 1/4 cup water and cornstarch together in a small bowl, stirring with a wire whisk until well blended—no lumps allowed. Add the cornstarch mixture and the petite peas to the slow cooker, stirring well to combine. Cover with lid and continue cooking on high setting for another 30 minutes.

Cook's Note: Correct seasonings if necessary and serve over big scoops of mashed potatoes.

Excerpted and adapted from The Frantic Family Cookbook (mostly) healthy meals in minutes ISBN 1189400118 by Leanne Ely, C.N.C.

Mrs. Stone's Green Bean Stew

6-8 servings

1-2 pounds pork shoulder
4 cups green beans, drained (preferably home canned)
1 medium onion, chopped fine
1/2 fresh green pepper, chopped fine
2 tablespoons butter
5-8 potatoes, peeled and sliced
2 cups stewed tomatoes
Salt and pepper to taste

Place pork shoulder in slow cooker with a little water. Cover with lid and simmer on high setting (approximately 5 hours) or until meat is tender. Remove meat from slow cooker and cool until you can easily pull meat from the bones. Set meat aside. Leave the pork water in the slow cooker. In a separate skillet melt the butter and sauté the onion and green pepper until tender. Add the sautéed vegetables, sliced potatoes, green beans and stewed tomatoes to the pork water in the slow cooker. Return the meat to the slow cooker, salt and pepper to taste, and let the stew simmer (covered) for 1 hour more, or until vegetables are very tender.

Excerpted and adapted from 365 Quick, Easy and Inexpensive Dinner Menus ISBN 1891400339 by Penny E. Stone

A Tip from the Kitchen...

When adding tender vegetables such as petite peas, zucchini and fresh mushrooms do so during the last 15 to 60 minutes of cooking. This will give your vegetables time to add flavor to the dish, without dissolving into mush from prolonged cooking. Their crisp-tender quality will add interest and texture to the completed dish.

Easy Hearty Beef Stew

6-8 servings

2 pounds stew beef, cut into 1-inch cubes
5 carrots cut into 1-inch cubes
1 large onion, cut into chunks
3 stalks celery, sliced
1 (28 ounce) can tomatoes
1/2 cup quick-cooking tapioca
1-2 whole cloves (or 1/2 teaspoon ground cloves)
2 bay leaves
Salt and pepper to taste

Trim all fat from meat. Put all ingredients into slow cooker. Mix thoroughly. Cover with lid and cook on low setting for 12 hours, or on high setting for 5-6 hours.

—from the kitchen of Joan Egan

A Tip from the Kitchen...

Raw root vegetables such as carrots, potatoes, parsnips and turnips hold their texture very well during prolonged cooking—in fact they tend to cook slower than the meat. A good rule is to place root vegetables in the bottom of the pot and nestle the meat on top for more even cooking.

Easy Casserole Stew

6-8 servings

2 pounds stew meat
4-5 carrots, chunked
3 onions, chunked
1 cup celery chunks
6 potatoes, halved
1 cup chopped green pepper
1 tablespoon sugar
2 tablespoons dry cornstarch
2 cups tomato juice
Salt and pepper to taste

Put first 6 ingredients in slow cooker. Mix together sugar and cornstarch and sprinkle into slow cooker. Add tomato juice. Cover with lid and cook on high setting for 4-6 hours, or until meat, potatoes and vegetables are very tender.

Recipe Contribution by MaryAnn Koopmann, Career Woman and Homemaker

A Tip from the Kitchen...

of *The Rush Hour Cook presents One Pot Wonders* by Brook Noel—For moister meats...When cooking soup or stew, replace water with wine, tea, broth or beer. Not only will experimenting with these liquids add delicious flavor, they will also help tenderize the meat.

Italiano Beef Stew

4 servings

1 pound lean beef, such as round steak
2 tablespoons olive oil
Salt and pepper to taste
1 (14.5 ounce) can stewed tomatoes, un-drained
2 teaspoons Italian seasoning, crushed
2 teaspoons garlic powder
1/8 teaspoon ground red pepper
3 medium carrots, cut in thin slices
3 small turnips, cut in 1/2 -inch slices, optional
1 large onion, chopped
2 tablespoons dry red wine, optional
1 (9 ounce) bag Italian (or pole) frozen green beans

In a Dutch oven, over medium-high heat, brown beef in the olive oil and season with salt and pepper. Put beef mixture in a slow cooker and add next 7 ingredients (canned tomatoes through onion). Cover with lid and cook on low setting for 5-6 hours. Increase the heat to high setting, and add wine and green beans (see note). Cover with lid and continue cooking until beans are tender. This stew recipe is equally good served with pasta or old-fashioned mashed potatoes.

Cook's Note: If adding beans still frozen, cooking time will increase significantly. Adding thawed beans will shorten cooking time. (See *Kitchen Tip* next page.)

Excerpted from The Frantic Family Cookbook (mostly) healthy meals in minutes ISBN 1189400118 by Leanne Ely, C.N.C.

A Tip from the Kitchen...

Adding frozen vegetables to your already simmering slow cooker can significantly increase cooking time by as much as 4 to 6 hours on low setting and 2 to 3 hours on high setting, depending on the amount added. A cup of frozen peas or corn won't matter much; but go easy on adding larger quantities of frozen items that will disrupt the cooking process. (You also risk cracking your crockery liner if the added-frozen food touches a hot side of the already heated and cooking pot!)

Catalina Beef Stew

6 servings

2 pounds stew beef, cut into cubes
1 (8 ounce) bottle Catalina® salad dressing
2 cups water
8-10 small potatoes, peeled and cubed
4-6 carrots, peeled and sliced
1/4 cup oil
1 ½ teaspoons salt
1/2 teaspoon black pepper

In shallow (non porous or glass) dish, pour Catalina® dressing over meat and set in refrigerator for at least 3 hours, or preferably overnight, to marinate. Remove meat from marinade and drain, reserving marinade. Pour marinade into slow cooker. In skillet heat oil and brown the meat pieces lightly on all sides. Drain the meat and add to slow cooker. Add remaining ingredients and stir to blend well. Cover with lid and cook on high setting for 5-6 hours, or on low setting for 7-9 hours. **Cook's Note:** Serve with biscuits.

Excerpted from Crazy About Crockery! 101 Soups and Stews ISBN 1891400126 by Penny E. Stone

A Tip from the Kitchen...

Inexpensive meats are perfect for slow cooking. Briskets, rump roasts, stew meat, shanks and short ribs, round steak and chuck roasts are all suitable for slow cooking. These tougher cuts of meat will be fork tender and very flavorful by the end of cooking time. And with less marbling of fat they will automatically provide leaner results. Take time to trim excess fat off the meat before placing in the slow cooker for even leaner results.

Lamb Stew
6-8 servings

3 pounds lean lamb, cut into bite-sized chunks
2 medium onions, finely chopped
1/2-1 pound fresh snow peas
1 (20 ounce) can stewed tomatoes
1 tablespoon honey
6-9 potatoes, peeled and cubed
1 teaspoon salt
1/2 teaspoon pepper
2 cups water
3 sprigs fresh parsley, chopped

Combine all ingredients in slow cooker. Cover with lid and cook on high setting for 4 hours. Reduce heat setting to low and continue cooking until you are ready to serve.

Excerpted from Crazy About Crockery! 101 Soups and Stews ISBN 1891400126 by Penny E. Stone

A Tip from the Kitchen...
"No, no, no...Don't peek!" Remember that every time you lift the lid on your slow cooker the steam escapes and the cooking temperature drops. One of the basic premises of slow cooker cooking is to surround the contents with hot steam and to maintain a slow, gentle, even temperature throughout. Every time you lift the lid it can take up to 15 to 20 minutes for the slow cooker to regain the lost steam and temperature!

Basic Beans
8 servings (of basic recipe-ready beans)

1 pound dried beans, rinsed and drained, picked clean
5 cups water, boiled

Put clean beans in your slow cooker. Bring a kettle to boil and pour 5 cups boiling water over the beans. Cover with lid and cook on high 3-4 hours, or on low 5-7 hours, depending on the size of the beans. When cooked, drain the beans well and rinse in a colander. Use for a recipe immediately, or store in freezer bags (labeled and dated) for a future recipe.

Excerpted from Healthy Foods, an irreverent guide to understanding nutrition and feeding your family well ISBN 1891400207 by Leanne Ely, C.N.C.

A Tip from the Kitchen...

Baking soda is the cleanser of choice for cleaning a stubborn crockery liner. Do not use abrasive cleansers that might damage the glazed finish. Let the liner soak with a little baking soda and warm water and your pot should come clean. And do not attempt to submerge the electrical-base unit into water! Clean off with a damp sponge. And always unplug while cleaning!

Sassy Baked Beans
6-8 servings

1 pound, dried Great Northern beans or navy beans
2 teaspoons baking soda
Water to cover
1 onion, diced
1 ½ cups tomato sauce
1/2 cup molasses
1/2 cup dark brown sugar
1 teaspoon dry mustard
1 teaspoon garlic powder
1 shot of Worcestershire sauce
Salt and pepper to taste

Bring water to a boil in large pot. While water is coming to a boil, in a colander, clean and rinse the beans. Add the beans to the boiling water and 'quick simmer' for 10 minutes. Remove from heat and stir in 2 teaspoons baking soda. Drain and rinse the beans. Place beans in slow cooker along with fresh water to cover. Cover with lid and cook on low heat 10-12 hours, or until fork tender. At this point drain off any excess cooking liquid until a cup or so remains. Blend remaining ingredients (diced onion through Worcestershire) mixing well, and stir into the beans. Cover and continue to cook on low setting for an additional 2-4 hours, until beans are hot and bubbly, thick and saucy, and cooked to your satisfaction. At the end of cooking adjust your seasonings with salt and pepper to taste.

Cook's Note: Incorporating salt into beans too soon can make them tough.—*from the kitchen of Wendy Louise*

Low Country Red Beans and Rice

8 servings

1 pound red beans, rinsed and cleaned
2 small onions, chopped
1 celery stalk, chopped
1 bell pepper, seeded and chopped
2 cloves garlic, pressed
1 cup water
3 cups chicken broth
1 ham hock (or substitute 1 smoked turkey leg)
1/2 teaspoon dried chili flakes (or more if you like heat)
Cooked brown rice, for serving

Using your crockery insert, soak the red beans overnight. In the morning drain beans, rinse and replace in slow cooker. Next, get out a large skillet; heat the oil over medium-high heat. Add celery, onion, bell pepper (Cajun cooks call this 'the holy trinity') and garlic. Cook until all is softened, about 5 minutes. Transfer this mixture to the slow cooker. Now add the chicken broth, water and ham hock (or turkey leg). Cover with lid and cook on low setting 8-10 hours. Before serving remove ham bone (or turkey leg) and chop the meat from the bone, discarding all fat and bone. Add meat back to slow cooker, along with hot chili flakes to taste. **Cook's Note:** Serve over brown rice with hot sauce or salsa and sour cream on the side.

Excerpted from The Frantic Family Cookbook (mostly) healthy meals in minutes ISBN 1189400118 by Leanne Ely, C.N.C.

Cowboy Beans
8 servings

1 pound pinto beans, rinsed, drained and picked over
5 cups water, boiled
2 onions, chopped
1 cup barbecue sauce (Hain® makes a good one)
2 squirts ketchup
1 carrot, grated
2 squirts mustard
Salt and pepper to taste
Additional bottle of barbecue sauce to serve on the side
  (optional)

In a slow cooker, mix beans, water, onion and carrot. Cover with lid and cook on high for 3-4 hours. Then cook on low for 7 hours or so. Drain beans and add the barbecue sauce, ketchup and mustard squirts. Salt and pepper to taste, mixing well, just before serving.

Cook's Note: Serve with plenty of cornbread (see buttermilk cornbread recipe, page 55) and honey butter on the side. Add a condiment of additional barbecue sauce on the table. A huge green salad completes the meal. "All you need is a campfire and a sleeve as your napkin."

Excerpted from Healthy Foods, an irreverent guide to understanding nutrition and feeding your family well ISBN 1891400207 by Leanne Ely, C.N.C.

Tex-Mex Chili

6 servings

3/4 pound ground beef (extra lean will keep the fat grams
  lower)
1 (15 ounce) can pinto beans
1 large onion, chopped
2 large cloves garlic, pressed
1 (14.5 ounce) can diced chilies, drained
1 (8.5 ounce) can whole kernel corn, un-drained
1 ½ teaspoons oregano
2 teaspoons cumin
Salt and pepper to taste
1/4 teaspoon cayenne pepper (optional)
2 tablespoons masa (corn flour, found in the ethnic section
  of the grocery store, used for making tortillas)

Brown beef; drain off fat and place in slow cooker. Next
add the rest of the ingredients (except the masa flour) and
stir to combine. Cover with lid and cook on low setting for
about 5 hours. Then, turn slow cooker to high setting.
While waiting for the slow cooker to heat up, stir 1/2 cup
cold water into the two tablespoons of masa and mix well
with a fork till fully incorporated. Add the masa mixture to
the slow cooker mixture, combining well, and allow to cook
for another hour. Serve in bowls topped with shredded
cheese, if desired.

*Excerpted from The Frantic Family Cookbook (mostly) healthy meals in
minutes ISBN 1189400118 by Leanne Ely, C.N.C.*

White Chicken Chili

6 servings

24 ounces canned white beans
2 cups chicken breast meat, cooked and cubed
1 cup chicken broth
2 medium onions, chopped
4 garlic cloves, minced
2 (4 ounce) cans chopped mild green chilies
1 teaspoon cumin
1 ½ teaspoons cayenne
Juice of a lime
Fresh cilantro, chopped coarsely

Combine all ingredients (except lime juice and cilantro). Cover with lid and cook on low for 8-10 hours (or on high for 4-5 hours). Just before serving, garnish with fresh lime juice and cilantro.

Excerpted and adapted from Frozen Assets Lite and Easy, cook for a day and eat for a month by Deborah Taylor-Hough ISBN 1 891400282

White Chili (with Pork)

6 servings

1/2 -1 pound boneless pork loin, cut into cubes
1 large onion, chopped
1 (16 ounce) can navy beans, drained
1 (16 ounce) can of chick peas, drained
1 (16 ounce) can of white kernel corn
1 (14.5 ounce) can chicken broth or chicken stock
1 cup cooked wild rice, or mixed grain rice
1 teaspoon ground cumin
Smashed and minced garlic cloves, to taste
A dash of hot sauce (optional)
Drained and diced canned chilies, to taste
A handful of white raisins

Brown the cubed pork and chopped onions in a little vegetable oil, until onions are soft and pork is lightly browned. Transfer the mixture to slow . Stir in remaining ingredients. Cover with lid and cook on low setting for at least 4 hours to meld flavors, but can simmer all day.
Cook's Note: Serve with shredded cheese (of your choice) and warmed flour tortillas.

-from the kitchen of Wendy Louise

A Tip from the Kitchen...

To warm tortillas wrap loosely in foil and heat in oven, or warm covered with a paper towel in the microwave. For a real treat warm them quickly, flipping on each side on a griddle. Bring to the table, covered in a towel-lined basket complete with a warming stone.

White Chili served with Buttermilk Cornbread

8 servings

2 pounds boneless, skinless chicken breasts, cut
  into bite-sized pieces
2 onions, chopped
2 1/2 cups chicken broth, canned or homemade
1 small can green chilies, chopped
1 can tomatillos
2 teaspoons each: cumin and garlic powder
1 teaspoon oregano
3 cups white beans, cooked, canned or make yourself
1/2 bunch cilantro, chopped (optional)
1 pound low-fat 'Jack cheese, grated

In a large saucepan, heat a small amount of oil and sauté
the onion. When the onion is translucent, add the chicken
pieces and cook a few minutes. Transfer to slow cooker and
add the rest of the ingredients, except for the cilantro and
the cheese. Cover with lid and cook on high for at least 3
hours. If you want it to cook all day, adjust the slow cooker
to low setting.

Cook's Note: Serve up the chili in big bowls, topped with a
sprinkling of cilantro and grated Jack cheese. Serve with
Buttermilk Cornbread (see recipe next page) and a big
salad.

Buttermilk Cornbread

Makes 10 servings

1 cup white cornmeal, use yellow if you can't find white

1 cup whole wheat pastry flour

1 ½ tablespoons Sucanat® (sugar substitute)

2 teaspoons baking powder

1/2 teaspoon baking soda

1/2 teaspoon sea salt

1 cup buttermilk

2 eggs, beaten

In a mixing bowl, toss together dry ingredients and make a well in the middle. In another bowl, mix beaten eggs and buttermilk together. Stir into the dry ingredients till moistened. Don't over mix! Pour batter into a greased 8-inch square pan. Bake in a preheated 425-degree oven until a toothpick inserted in the middle comes out clean, approximately 18 to 20 minutes. **Cook's Note:** Do not over cook! Cut into squares and serve fresh and warm with the chili.

Excerpted from Healthy Foods, an irreverent guide to understanding nutrition and feeding your family well ISBN 1891400207 by Leanne Ely, C.N.C.

A Tip from the Kitchen...

When adding canned or preserved ingredients to your recipes go easy on the salt. You may not have to add any! If needed, adjust seasonings to your liking toward end of cooking time.

Ham and Beans

8 servings

Cook's Note: This recipe requires some advanced preparation the night before cooking, but makes a great winter-weekend meal.

1 pound soup beans
Water to cover
2 teaspoons baking soda
2 tablespoons vinegar
1 tablespoon dried parsley flakes
2 smoked ham hocks
Additional ham, chunked
Salt and pepper, to taste

To prepare soup beans, wash, rinse, and then soak overnight in water. The next morning rinse beans again and cover with water and bring to a fast boil. Remove from heat and add 2 teaspoons of baking soda and stir. Drain the beans in a colander and rinse again. Your beans are now ready to be used in the recipe. Put the beans in the slow cooker and cover with fresh water. Add the vinegar, parsley flakes, smoked ham hocks, and additional ham (if desired). Do not salt and pepper at this time. (Penny Stone suggests, "Never add salt to beans until you are ready to serve them. The salt will make the beans tough.") Cover with lid and cook all day on high heat, or for at least 8 hours. When ready to serve, salt and pepper to taste. **Cook's Note:** Serve with corn bread and a salad.

Excerpted from 365 Quick, Easy and Inexpensive Dinner Menus ISBN 1891400339 by Penny E. Stone

A Tip from the Kitchen...

To stay organized, read through your complete recipe, start to finish, **before** you start cooking. Make sure you understand all the steps involved and have all your ingredients on hand **before** you begin–and cooking will be a breeze.

A Tip from the Kitchen...

Need an impromptu gift? Have a friend convalescing at home? Know a mom just returning with a new born? Need a quick hostess gift for a last minute party?—Why not give a homemade sauce, chutney or compote, straight from your own kitchen!—Check out the Rush Hour Cook's gift-basket-idea on page 103. For more applicable ideas (and how to sterilize containers) see pages 205-207. Be sure to include a decorative card, along with your original recipe and serving suggestions. I can't think of anyone who wouldn't appreciate the luxury of ... "a little already-made, comfort-food from a friend, creatively presented in such a decorative and thoughtful manner."

Chapter Two:
Come and Get It!
Everyday Entrees

"Come and get it..." A main stay to our family's diet, everyday meals make up the majority of our cooking. We all have our favorites and our 'tried-and-trues' but once in a while it's fun to add a new recipe to our collection. So "come and get it"... we have everything from Chicken in a Pot to Lazy Day Roast in this chapter.

Everyday Entrees Chapter Index

Old Fashioned Chicken and Rice

6 servings

2 ½ cups chicken broth
1 ½ pounds boneless skinless chicken breast meat, cut into 1-inch pieces or strips
1 ½ cups long grain rice, uncooked
1 cup chopped onion

1/4 cup fresh parsley, minced
6 garlic cloves, minced
1 small red bell pepper, cut into thin strips
1 (6 ounce) jar sliced mushrooms, un-drained

Combine all ingredients in slow cooker. Cover with lid and cook on high setting for 3-4 hours, or until chicken is no longer pink and rice is plumped and tender.

Excerpted and adapted from Frozen Assets Lite and Easy, cook for a day and eat for a month by Deborah Taylor-Hough ISBN 1 891400282

Chicken "Broccoli Bake" Variation

6 servings

Exchange the red bell pepper (in the above recipe) for 1 (16 ounce) bag of frozen broccoli pieces, thawed and also fold in the addition of 1 (10.75 ounce) can of cream Cheddar cheese soup (undiluted). Omit poultry seasoning, but add salt and pepper to taste. Cover with lid and cook on high setting for 4 hours, or until chicken is done, rice is plumped and broccoli is fork tender. —*from the kitchen of Wendy Louise*

Salsa-fied-Chicken

6 servings

6 boneless, skinless chicken breasts
1 ½ cups chunky style salsa
1 (14.5 ounce) can of corn, drained
1 (14.5 ounce) can of black beans, rinsed and drained
Salt and pepper to taste

Lightly salt and pepper chicken breasts and place in slow cooker. Mix corn, black beans and salsa, and pour over chicken. Cover with lid and cook on low setting 6-8 hours, or 2-4 hours on high setting, adding a little broth if necessary.

Cook's Note: Serve with warmed tortillas or rice, and additional salsa for garnish. (See warming tortillas, page 53 and Spastic Salsa, page 160.)

Excerpted from Crazy About Crockery! 101 easy and inexpensive recipes for less than .75 cents a serving by Penny E Stone ISBN 1891400126

A Tip from the Kitchen...

You'll notice that this recipe calls for lightly seasoning the chicken with salt and pepper...During extended-style cooking, seasonings can tend to intensify. It is very easy to over season! A wise idea is to adjust seasonings to your taste near the end of cooking. If you need to 'save' a dish a raw potato can be added to soak up some of the seasoning. Remove the potato before serving, and no one will ever know...

Colorful Cheddar Chicken

6-8 servings

1 whole chicken, cut up, skin removed
1 cup water
8 slices dried bread, torn into pieces
1/2 cup chopped celery
1 onion, chopped, or 6-8 green onions, chopped
1/2 cup mayonnaise
1/2 cup green pepper, chopped
1 small can of pimentos, chopped and drained
2 cups shredded sharp Cheddar cheese
1 can cream of mushroom soup
1 soup can water
1 cup chopped carrots

Rub each piece of chicken with mayonnaise. Combine chicken, water, celery, onion, green pepper and carrots in slow cooker. Cover with lid and cook on high setting for 6-7 hours. Remove chicken and add all remaining ingredients to slow cooker. Stir to blend well. Return chicken to slow cooker. Cover with lid, reduce heat setting to low and continue cooking for another 1-2 hours.

Excerpted from Crazy About Crockery! 101 easy and inexpensive recipes for less than .75 cents a serving by Penny E Stone ISBN 1891400126

A Tip from the Kitchen...

You'll notice in this recipe that Penny has added the cheese during the last portion of cooking time. Like other dairy products, cheeses have a tendency to hold up better if added toward the end of cooking or by reducing the setting to low.

Leanne's Double Duty Chicken

12 servings

1 large roasting chicken
1 onion
1 carrot
1 celery rib
4 cloves garlic
1 teaspoon thyme
Salt and pepper to taste

Wash and dry chicken and place in slow cooker. Break whole carrot and celery rib into halves and place in the cavity of the chicken. Cut the onion into halves and place, along with the garlic cloves, into the cavity of the chicken. Don't add any water. Cover with lid and cook on high setting for about 4 hours. **Cook's Note:** You should have a heavenly smell coming from your kitchen and double rich chicken broth. Remove chicken from the slow cooker. When it has cooled, de-bone, degrease and skin it, and chop the meat. Use in your favorite recipe calling for cooked chicken meat; or put in a zip-top freezer bag, label and date, and store in the freezer for future use. Strain the broth into a bowl and refrigerate for a few hours. Remove the congealed fat off the top and discard. Use the broth for a favorite recipe; or freeze, label and date for future use.

Excerpted from Healthy Foods, an irreverent guide to understanding nutrition and feeding your family well ISBN 1891400207 by Leanne Ely, C.N.C.

A Tip from the Kitchen...

You'll notice on the previous page that Leanne had not added any broth or water to her recipe—A great advantage to crockery cooking is the fact that the slow cooker utilizes the moisture already inherent in the ingredients, by returning the accumulating steam back down into the meat and vegetables. It is important to snugly secure the lid on the pot, so these precious juices do not escape and to refrain from lifting the lid any more than necessary.

Joan's "Chicken in a Pot"

6-8 servings

1 (3 pound) chicken, left whole
2 carrots, sliced
2 onions, sliced
2 celery stalks, with leaves, cut into 1-inch pieces
2 teaspoons salt
1/2 teaspoon black pepper
1/2-1 teaspoon crushed basil
1/2 cup water, chicken broth or white wine

Put vegetables in bottom of slow cooker. Salt and pepper the chicken and put on top of the vegetables. Pour in the 1/2 cup liquid and sprinkle with basil. Cover with lid and cook on low setting 7-10 hours (or 2 ½ -3 ½ hours on high setting, adding another 1/2 cup liquid). Carefully remove chicken from the slow cooker, using a spatula. Strain juices and make gravy.

—from the kitchen of Joan Egan

Chicken 'Pattow'

6 servings

6 boneless, skinless chicken breasts, frozen
1 box stuffing mix
1 can cream of chicken or cream of mushroom soup
1 cup frozen peas

Place stuffing mix (with its seasonings) on the bottom of the slow cooker. Top with frozen peas and frozen chicken breasts. Pour soup over top of chicken and cook on low setting all day. Stuffing will be moist from the peas, chicken and soup.

Cook's Note: If you want to shorten the cooking time of this recipe start with thawed peas and thawed chicken and proceed with the recipe. (See *Kitchen Tip* on page 44 for information on frozen foods.)

—*from the kitchen of Sara Pattow*

Almond Classic Chicken

6 servings

1 whole chicken, cut up, skin removed
2 cups water, divided
1 large onion, chopped
1 teaspoon salt
1/2 -3/4 teaspoon black pepper, depending upon taste
3 stalks celery, diced
1 (10 ounce) package frozen peas, thawed
1 (4 ounce) can sliced mushrooms, drained
2 tablespoons cornstarch
1/2 teaspoon ground ginger
3 tablespoons soy sauce
1/2 -1 cup toasted slivered almonds

Arrange chicken pieces in slow cooker. Scatter chopped onion and celery over the meat. Sprinkle with salt and pepper and add 1 ½ cups of the water. Cover with lid and cook on high for 5 hours. Remove chicken from slow cooker and let cool. To the remaining juices add thawed peas and the mushrooms. Dissolve the cornstarch in remaining 1/2 cup cold water and pour into the slow cooker. Add the ginger, soy sauce and toasted-slivered almonds. Pick chicken off the bones and tear into bite-sized pieces. Add meat back into slow cooker and stir to blend well. Cover with lid and reduce heat setting to low. Continue cooking for 2 hours on low setting to allow flavors to blend. **Cook's Note:** Serve over cooked rice.

Excerpted from Crazy About Crockery! 101 easy and inexpensive recipes for less than.75 cents a serving by Penny E Stone ISBN 1891400126

Creamy Chicken, Broccoli and Rice Casserole

6 servings

1 whole chicken, cut into pieces, skin removed

3 cups water

2 teaspoons salt

2 cups instant rice, uncooked

1 onion, chopped

3 tablespoons butter, melted

1/4 cup flour

1 ½ cups half-and-half cream

2 tablespoons chopped parsley

1/2 teaspoon black pepper

1 package chopped frozen broccoli, thawed

1/2 cup slivered almonds

Place chicken into slow cooker with water and 1 teaspoon salt. Cover with lid and cook on high setting for 6 hours. After chicken is cooked, remove chicken from slow cooker and set aside. Pour cooking liquid into a large measuring cup and reserve. In a saucepan, melt butter and sauté onions and almonds until onions are transparent. Add flour and stir to make a paste. Add the half-and-half and reserved chicken broth and continue cooking over medium-high heat until mixture forms a smooth gravy. Pour mixture back into slow cooker. De-bone the chicken meat and return to the sauce in the slow cooker. Add all remaining ingredients and stir to blend well. Cover with lid and continue cooking on high setting for 2-4 more hours.

Excerpted from Crazy About Crockery! 101 easy and inexpensive recipes for less than .75 cents a serving by Penny E Stone ISBN 1891400126

Round Steak Casserole

6-8 servings

2 pounds round steak, cut 1/2-inch thick
Garlic salt, salt and pepper to taste
1 onion, thinly sliced
3-4 potatoes, peeled and quartered (optional)
1 can French-style green beans, drained
1 (10 ounce) can tomato soup
1 (16 ounce) can tomatoes (peeled and whole)

Season round steak lightly with salt, pepper and garlic salt. Cut into serving-size pieces and place in slow cooker with sliced onion which has been separated into rings. Add potatoes (if using) and green beans. Top with tomato soup and tomatoes. Cover with lid and cook on low setting for 8 hours. Remove cover during last half-hour of cooking to reduce liquid if necessary.

—from the kitchen of Joan Egan

A Tip from the Kitchen...

of June Kirzan—When using tomatoes in soups, stews and sauces, the addition of a little sugar or baking soda offsets their acidity.

Chili Steak

6 servings

2 pounds (or more) round steak
1 large onion, chopped
1 teaspoon salt
1/4 teaspoon black pepper
2 cups prepared chili sauce, or 2 cups homemade chili sauce
2 cups water

Place the onions on the bottom of the slow cooker. Cut the meat into serving-sized slices and place onto the onions in the slow cooker. Sprinkle meat with salt and pepper. Add the chili sauce and water. Cover with lid and cook on low setting for 7 hours, or until meat is fork tender.

Cook's Note: Serve over baked potatoes, topped with Cheddar cheese.

Excerpted from Crazy About Crockery! 101 Recipes for Entertaining at less than .75 cents a serving ISBN 1891400525 by Penny E. Stone

Glenn's Beef and Beer

6 servings

2 pounds stew meat
1 cup flour
4 tablespoons salad oil
2 cans beef consommé
1/4 teaspoon each: thyme, oregano, garlic powder, onion
  powder
1 can beer
1 bay leaf

Dredge meat in flour; brown in oil. Put meat in slow cooker and cover with soup, seasonings and beer. Cover and cook on low setting for 8-10 hours.

—from the kitchen of Glenn Koopmann

Cook's Note: Serve over rice, noodles or mashed potatoes for a hearty no-fuss, no-muss main dish.

Braised Beef

6 servings

1 tablespoon olive oil

2 pounds lean boneless beef, cut into 1-inch cubes, trimmed of fat

4 cups chopped onion

4 cups chopped carrots

1-2 garlic cloves, minced

1 cup dry red wine

1 bay leaf

1 teaspoon crushed oregano

1 teaspoon thyme

Salt and pepper to taste

In skillet brown the beef and cook the onions (until transparent) in the olive oil. Transfer to slow cooker. Top with carrots and garlic. Pour in wine and add seasonings. Add bay leaf. Cover with lid and cook on low setting at least 6 hours, or until meat is very tender. Add additional wine or water if necessary. Remove bay leaf before serving.

Cook's Note: Serve with a potato dish of your choice and a fresh vegetable or salad.

Excerpted and adapted from Frozen Assets Lite and Easy, cook for a day and eat for a month with Deborah Taylor-Hough ISBN 1 891400282

A Tip from the Kitchen…

The keys to a well rounded meal are variety and contrast—A complex dish with a simple salad. A spicy dish accompanied with something cool or sweet. A slow cooked dish along with fresh fruit. Plan your meals to incorporate contrasting textures, colors and tastes. You will find that many of these recipes include Cook's Notes, offering serving suggestions to help you.

Beef Roast with Onion-Mushroom Gravy

6-8 servings

3 to 4 pound beef roast, trimmed of excess fat
1 envelope dry onion soup mix
2 tablespoons A-1 Sauce®
2 cans cream of mushroom soup
1 soup can water
1 onion, chopped
2 cups fresh sliced mushrooms
Salt and pepper to taste

Place roast in slow cooker. Combine next 5 ingredients and pour over roast. Cover with lid and cook on high setting for 7-9 hours. Add sliced mushrooms last hour of cooking and adjust seasoning to taste with salt and pepper.

Excerpted from The Rush Hour Cook presents Effortless Entertaining ISBN 189140086X by Brook Noel

Lazy Day Roast

6 servings

2 pounds round steak,
  cubed
2 large onions, finely
  chopped
1 tablespoon Worcestershire
  sauce
1 large can tomato soup
3 carrots, sliced
1 tablespoon bread crumbs
1 tablespoon tapioca

1 tablespoon vinegar
1 can peas
2 tablespoons sugar
1 ½ cups water
1 tablespoon salt
1 teaspoon whole pepper
  corns
4 bay leaves
4 whole cloves

Combine all ingredients (except bay leaves and cloves) and place in large slow cooker. On top place 4 bay leaves and 4 cloves. Cover and cook on high setting at least 4 hours, or until meat is fork tender. Remove bay leaves and cloves before serving.

Recipe contribution by MaryAnn Koopmann, Career Woman and Homemaker

A Tip from the Kitchen...

In this recipe MaryAnn has used whole spices to season her dish. In extended slow cooking, whole spices hold up better than crushed, while infusing generous amounts of flavor. Be sure to remove the whole spices before serving. You can tie your spices in a little bag of cheese cloth for easy removal.

Easy-Style Homemade Pot Roast of Beef

6-8 servings

1 (3-4 pound) brisket, rump roast, or pot roast
2-3 potatoes, peeled and sliced
2-3 carrots, peeled and sliced
1-2 onions, peeled and sliced
1/2 cup water or beef consommé
Salt and pepper to taste

Put vegetables in slow cooker. Salt and pepper the meat and place on top of the vegetables. Add the water or consommé. Cover with lid and cook on low setting for 10-12 hours, or high setting 4-5 hours. Remove roast to a deep dish platter and slice before serving. Surround with vegetables and cooking juices.

Variations:

German-style: Add 3-4 medium dill pickles and 1 teaspoon dill weed to the above recipe.

Italian-style: Add 1 (8 ounce) can tomato sauce, 1 teaspoon crushed oregano and 1 teaspoon basil to the above recipe.

French-style: Omit carrots and potatoes. Add 1 cup fresh sliced mushrooms, or 1 (8 ounce) can of sliced mushrooms. Use 1 pound small peeled onions, or pearl onions. Add 1 cup dry red wine.

Basic Pot Roast-Plain and Simple: Season roast with salt and pepper and any other favorite seasonings. Place in slow cooker. Do not add any vegetables or liquid in this version. Cover with lid and cook on low setting 10-12 hours, or until meat is extremely tender.

—from the kitchen of Joan Egan

Crock Roast

10 servings

1 (3 pound) rump roast, trimmed
Salt and pepper to taste
3 cloves garlic
2 teaspoons thyme
1 onion, quartered
4 carrots, sliced 1-inch thick
1/2 cup beef broth
1 cup dry red wine (or additional broth)

In a large skillet, brown beef on all sides. Salt and pepper to taste. Transfer the roast to slow cooker and top with thyme. Put carrots, onions and garlic cloves over and around roast. In the skillet that browned the beef, add the wine and broth and cook till boiling, deglazing the pan. Pour this on top of the beef and vegetables in the slow cooker. Cover with lid and cook on high setting for about 4-5 hours, or until beef is extremely tender. Or cook covered on low setting all day. Adjust seasoning of salt and pepper to taste at end of cooking, if necessary.

Excerpted from Healthy Foods, an irreverent guide to understanding nutrition and feeding your family well ISBN 1891400207 by Leanne Ely, C.N.C.

Simple Swiss Steak

6 servings

2 pounds round or Swiss steak, cut 3/4-inch thick
Salt and pepper to taste
1 large onion, thinly sliced
1 (16 ounce) can tomatoes, with juice

Cut round steak into serving-size pieces and season with salt and pepper. Place in slow cooker with sliced onion. Pour tomatoes over all. Cover with lid and cook on low setting for 8-10 hours.

—from the kitchen of Joan Egan

Creamy Swiss Steak

6 servings

Substitute 1 (10 ounce) can of mushroom soup in place of the tomatoes and you have turned Simple Swiss Steak (above) into Creamy Swiss Steak.

—from the kitchen of Joan Egan

Hungarian Round Steak

6 servings

2-3 pounds lean round steak, cut into serving portions
2 large onions, chopped
1 clove garlic, minced
2 quarts canned whole tomatoes
1/2 cup flour
1 teaspoon salt
1/2 teaspoon coarsely ground pepper
1 teaspoon paprika
1/2 teaspoon dried thyme
1 bay leaf

Dredge meat in flour and place in slow cooker. Add onions and garlic. Cut and chop tomatoes then pour into slow cooker. Add seasonings. Cover with lid and cook on high setting for 6 hours. Remove bay leaf before serving.

Cook's Note: The tomato-based sauce makes an excellent gravy over cooked noodles or rice.

Excerpted from Crazy About Crockery! 101 easy and inexpensive recipes for less than .75 cents a serving by Penny E Stone ISBN 1891400126

A Tip from the Kitchen...

of Penny E. Stone, *Crazy About Crockery!* "To avoid the possibility of food poisoning, don't store leftover food in your slow cooker. Always transfer crockery contents to a suitable container and refrigerate or freeze immediately after serving."

Miss Kim's Short Ribs and Dumplings in a Pot

6-8 servings

4 pounds of short ribs, rinsed and patted dry
2 cans of beef broth
1 (broth) can of water
6 carrots, sliced down the middle
6 potatoes, washed, peeled and left whole
1 large tomato, chopped
Salt, pepper and garlic to taste

Place all ingredients in slow cooker. Cover with lid and cook on low setting for 8-10 hours, or until meat is very tender, and vegetables and potatoes are done. Serve with dumplings (see below).

Dumplings:
   2 cups Bisquick®
   2/3 cup milk
Turn slow cooker setting to high. Stir Bisquick® and milk together to form a moist batter, but don't over mix. Drop by tablespoonfuls onto the bubbling liquid, cover and cook on high setting for 10 minutes. Uncover and continue cooking for 10 minutes more, or until dumplings are fully cooked.

Cook's Note: Add garlic bread and a dessert of lemon sherbet for a complete meal.

—from the kitchen of Kim Meiloch, who's both nurtured and nourished many a child

L.J.'s Barbecued Ribs

6 servings

4 pounds back ribs, cut into serving size portions of 3-4
  ribs each
Salt and pepper
1 onion, sliced into rings
1 (16 ounce) bottle of smoky barbecue sauce, or your
  favorite flavor, or 2 cups of homemade sauce

Sprinkle ribs with salt and pepper and place in slow cooker
with onion rings. Pour on the sauce. Cover with lid and
cook on low setting for 6-8 hours, or high setting 3-4 hours.

—*Recipe submitted by Joan Egan*

Barbecue-in-a-Pot Beef
8 servings

1 (3 pound) round roast, chuck roast (or whatever you find
  on sale)
1 ½ cups barbecue sauce
8 hamburger buns

Heat the oil in your skillet and brown the beef roast on all
sides. Salt and pepper liberally and place in a slow cooker.
Cover with lid and cook on low setting for 8-10 hours.
Remove roast from slow cooker and let rest about 10
minutes. Either slice thinly or shred with forks and place
open faced on hamburger buns. Reserve sauce from
cooking (you may need to skim some of the fat off the top)
and use for dipping.

 Cook's Note: Delicious served with a side of coleslaw or a
salad.

*Excerpted from The Frantic Family Cookbook (mostly) healthy meals in
minutes ISBN 1189400118 by Leanne Ely, C.N.C.*

BBQ'S
6 servings

2-3 pounds round steak, trimmed of fat and cut into cubes
3-4 tablespoons brown sugar
2 teaspoons salt
3 tablespoons Worcestershire sauce
1 tablespoon vinegar
1/4 teaspoon each dill, chives, parsley, sweet basil, dry
    mustard
1 cup water
1 tablespoon grape jelly
2 tablespoons cornstarch, dissolved in 1/2 cup water

Place cubed meat in slow cooker. Mix the rest of ingredients together, stirring well and pour over meat. Stir again well to coat all. Cover with lid and cook on low setting for 5-7 hours, or until meat is very tender. Serve the meat and sauce on rolls. (Can shred the meat if desired.)

—from the kitchen of Kim Mieloch, fondly referred to, by many a child, as
"Miss Kim"

A Tip from the Kitchen...
Using dark brown sugar in your recipes adds depth and a nice caramelizing flavor to sauces and glazes.

Sloppy Joes
6 servings

1 pound lean ground beef
1 (8 ounce) can tomato sauce
1 tablespoon Worcestershire sauce
1 green pepper, diced
1 yellow onion, diced
1 teaspoon salt
1/4 teaspoon pepper
1 teaspoon Italian seasoning
1 teaspoon dried oregano
1 teaspoon dried sweet basil
1/2 teaspoon garlic powder

Brown meat in skillet, along with onion and green pepper.
Drain off excess fat and transfer to slow cooker. Stir in
tomato sauce, Worcestershire sauce and all seasonings,
mixing well. Cover with lid and simmer on low setting for 1-
2 hours (3-4 hours if tripling the recipe). Can hold
indefinitely.

Cook's Note: Scoop right out of the slow cooker and serve
warm on bread or buns. Or at Penny's suggestion, serve
with her Homemade Potato Wedges (see next page).

*Excerpted and adapted from 365 Quick, Easy and Inexpensive Dinner Menus
ISBN 1891400339 by Penny E. Stone*

A Tip from the Kitchen...
This is a good time to remind you (as I mentioned in the
introduction) to "Turn off and Unplug" your base unit
before you remove the liner to the table for direct serving.

Penny's Homemade Potato Wedges

6 servings

6-8 potatoes, scrubbed clean. Leave skins intact.
3 tablespoons olive oil
Vegetable spray
Seasoned salt
Grated Parmesan cheese

Line a large cookie sheet with aluminum foil. Spread with olive oil. Cut potatoes into wedges and place skin-side down on the prepared baking sheet. Spray the wedges with vegetable spray and sprinkle with seasoned salt and grated Parmesan cheese. Bake for 45 minutes in a 400-degree oven. Check for tenderness. Wedges may need to bake an additional 15 minutes, depending upon how soft you like them.

Cook's Note: Serve along side Sloppy Joes (see previous page).

Excerpted and adapted from 365 Quick, Easy and Inexpensive Dinner Menus ISBN 1891400339 by Penny E. Stone

Crockery Taco Meat

10 plus servings

1 (3 pound) bottom round beef roast
Salt and pepper to taste
1 cup water
1 tablespoon cumin
1 tablespoon garlic powder
2 teaspoons oregano
1 teaspoon sea salt

In a skillet, over medium heat, brown the beef on all sides in a little oil. Salt and pepper to taste. Transfer to the slow cooker. In a small bowl, mix together the cumin, garlic powder, oregano and sea salt. Set aside.

Deglaze your skillet with 1 cup of water, vigorously stirring up all the tasty tidbits in the pan. Let simmer until reduced by half; then pour over the roast. Sprinkle half the mixed seasonings over the roast. Cover with lid and cook the roast on low setting for 8-10 hours, until very tender. Remove the meat from the slow cooker and let cool enough to handle. Shred the meat with a fork and place in a bowl. Sprinkle with the remaining half of seasonings, mixing well. Cover bowl and keep meat warm while the flavors meld (or return to the slow cooker until serving time).

Cook's Note: Serve with warmed tortillas, black beans, brown rice and all the fixings you desire.

Excerpted from Healthy Foods, an irreverent guide to understanding nutrition and feeding your family well ISBN 1891400207 by Leanne Ely, C.N.C.

Sara's 'Busta Move' Beef Taco Meat

6 servings

1 pound ground beef
1 onion, chopped
1 teaspoon chili powder
1 teaspoon pepper
1 tablespoon hot sauce (Sara's signature ingredient)
1 teaspoon salt
1/4 cup salsa (heat—your choice, mild, medium or hot)
1/4 cup taco sauce
1/2 cup refried beans

Brown ground beef and onions in skillet, drain fat and put in slow cooker. Stir in all remaining ingredients and cook on low setting for 8 hours. *–from the kitchen of Sara Pattow*

Cook's Note: Serve in taco shells (soft or hard), or as meat on nachos, or in taco salads. Recipe may be doubled.

A Tip from the Kitchen...

Remember that slow cookers cook optimally when at least 1/2 full—but on the other hand, not more than 3/4 full. Sometimes you have to customize the pot size to the recipe, or the recipe size to the available pot. This is especially important when cooking for an extended or unattended period of time.

Polish Sausage and 'Kraut

6 servings

2 pounds Polish sausage, cut into serving pieces
1 (16 ounce) can sauerkraut, with juice
2 teaspoons caraway seeds
1-2 tablespoons brown sugar
8-10 small potatoes, peeled (or preferably washed red
  potatoes with skins left on)
Water

Empty un-drained can of sauerkraut into the slow cooker.
Sprinkle with caraway seeds and brown sugar. Stir to mix.
Add raw potatoes and sausage pieces. Cover all with water.
Cover with lid and cook on low setting for 7-8 hours.

*Excerpted and adapted for slow cooker-style- cooking, from 365 Quick, Easy
and Inexpensive Dinner Menus ISBN 1891400339 by Penny E. Stone*

A Tip from the Kitchen...

When using meats, sausages (and the like) take the time to
brown them first in a skillet with a little diced onion before
adding to slow cooker. You can also 'deglaze' the pan to
pickup extra added bits of flavor, putting those juices in the
slow cooker as well. If you prefer not to brown your meats
first, the addition of a little Kitchen Bouquet® can enhance
and enrich the flavors of the finished dish. Kitchen
Bouquet® is a richly concentrated bottled-flavoring sauce.
You can usually find it in the condiment or specialty-food
aisle of your market. Use it to enhance color, flavors and
depth.

Your Choice Pork Chops

Brown chops well, season lightly with salt and pepper and place in slow cooker. Cover with **one** of the following sauces:

   1 can cream of mushroom soup

   1 can cream of chicken soup

   1 jar sweet and sour sauce

   1-2 cups jarred barbecue sauce

Cover with lid and cook on low setting 6-8 hours.

Cook's Note: Four choices in one simple recipe! How easy is that!

—*from the kitchen of Joan Egan*

Apple Chops
4 servings

4 pork chops

2 apples, sliced

1 cup rice, uncooked

1 onion, finely chopped

1 stalk celery, diced

1 teaspoon each: rosemary, thyme, salt and pepper

1 cup water or apple cider

Brown chops on each side for 3 minutes. Set aside. Place rice, onion celery and seasonings in slow cooker, mixing well. Top with apple slices and then browned chops. Pour in 1 cup water or cider. Cover with lid and cook on low setting for 6-8 hours. Recipe may be doubled for larger crockery pot.

—*Recipe submitted by Joan Egan*

Mambone's Pork Chops
6-8 servings

6-8 lean pork chops, about 1-inch thick
1/2 cup flour
1 teaspoon salt
1 ½ teaspoons dry mustard
1/2 teaspoon garlic powder
2 tablespoons oil
1 can chicken and rice soup

Mix flour and seasonings. Dredge pork chops in the flour mixed with seasonings. Brown in oil in a large skillet. Place the browned chops into the slow cooker. Add the can of soup. Cover with lid and cook on low for 6-8 hours, or high setting 3 ½ hours. Serve with applesauce.

—*Recipe submitted by that "Pork Chop Gal", Joan Egan*

A Tip from the Kitchen...

Pork chops—an often overlooked yet versatile "other white meat" can usually be bought inexpensively in on-the-bone, family-style packs. On-the-bone chops add extra flavor to the dish. Children love pork —and applesauce on the side offers them a 'reprieve' from tossed salad and the 'dreaded vegetable'. So serve up some 'chops and 'sauce for a kid-friendly treat. (See applesauce recipes, pages 203-204.)

Provencal Pork
6 servings

2 pounds boneless pork chops, cut into 1/2 -inch thick
  strips
1/4 cup butter
2 medium onions, sliced
1 (15 ounce) can of stewed tomatoes (with juice)
1 ½ pounds potatoes, thinly sliced
1/2 to 1 teaspoon dried mixed herbs
Salt and pepper to taste
Freshly chopped parsley (for garnish)

In a large skillet, over medium heat, melt half the butter.
Add strips of pork and cook until lightly browned. Remove
pork from pan and reserve. Add the onion to the pan and
cook until translucent. Mix in tomatoes, their juice, salt,
pepper and mixed-herbs to form a sauce. In a slow cooker
layer pork, then sauce, then potato slices. Repeat layers,
ending with potatoes on top. Dot the top layer of potatoes
with remaining butter. Cover with lid and cook on low
setting 6-8 hours, or until pork is thoroughly cooked and
potatoes are tender. Garnish with fresh parsley at serving
time.

*Excerpted and adapted from Frozen Assets Lite and Easy, cook for a day and
eat for a month by Deborah Taylor-Hough ISBN 1 891400282*

A Tip from the Kitchen...
When using dried herbs (such as parsley, oregano, thyme,
basil, etc.) crumble them between your fingers to release
extra flavor.

Roast Pork with Vegetables

6-8 servings

1 (3 pound) boneless pork loin roast
1-3 cloves garlic, peeled
1 large onion, sliced
6 medium potatoes
6 carrots cut in 1-inch chunks
1 teaspoon salt
1/2 teaspoon pepper
1 bay leaf
3/4 cup apple juice

Rub the pork roast thoroughly with the garlic cloves and then place roast in the slow cooker. Arrange the onions, carrots and potatoes under and around the roast. Sprinkle on the salt and pepper; add the bay leaf; and throw in the garlic cloves for good measure. Drizzle on the apple juice. Cover with lid and cook on low setting for 8 hours, or until meat is fork tender. Carefully remove roast and vegetables from slow cooker to a warm platter. Discard the garlic cloves and bay leaf. Turn slow cooker to high setting. Mix 1 tablespoon cornstarch with 1 tablespoon water and add to crockery juices to make gravy. Cook on high (uncovered) until gravy thickens. Slice pork roast just before serving and drizzle gravy over all.

—*from the kitchen of Wendy Louise*

A Tip from the Kitchen...

Infusing garlic —Slits may be cut in the meat and the peeled garlic cloves inserted directly into the roast for added flavor.

Penny's Pork Roast with Vegetables

6 servings

1 (3-4 pound) pork roast, leave fat intact
1 onion, quartered or sliced
6-9 medium potatoes, peeled
4-6 large carrots cut in thirds
2 packets brown or pork gravy mix
2 cups water
Additional salt and pepper to taste, if necessary

Place meat in slow cooker, fat side up. Arrange vegetables around meat. In saucepan, prepare gravy packets with water according to package directions. Pour over meat and vegetables in slow cooker. Cover with lid and cook on high setting for 7-9 hours. Adjust seasoning if necessary.

Excerpted from Crazy About Crockery! 101 easy and inexpensive recipes for less than .75 cents a serving by Penny E Stone ISBN 1891400126

A Tip from the Kitchen...

When using seasoning packets, gravy packets and the like, go lightly on your own seasoning of salt and pepper. Adjust to your taste at end of cooking if necessary. This 'rule of thumb' can be applied to canned goods also; more than often they contain enough salt on their own, to satisfy your palate.

A Tip from the Kitchen...

Want to thicken your sauce, soup or gravy?—A great way to do this is to remove a portion of your cooked vegetables and puree them in the blender; then blend the pureed mixture back into the cooking juices, incorporating until smooth. For an extra touch you can puree the cooked vegetables with a little wine, sherry, port or apple juice for extra flavor, and then add back to the pot. In the beginning, when you are assembling your recipe, add some extra vegetables to the pot just for this purpose.

Chapter Three:
What's Cookin'?

'Hand-Me-Down' Entrees

"What's cookin'..." is a special section devoted to "inherited recipes" from family members and friends. As a child I grew up way before the electric slow cooker was invented and have fond memories of "from-scratch" recipes simmering on the stove or cooking in the oven... I can still picture my mother standing over the stove, tending to her favorite recipes. The aromas when I came home from school were so inviting and her love and affection, shown to me through cooking, were wonderful gifts.

I think you'll find that you too have similar recipes tucked away in your recipe box. I call them "hand-me-downs". With a little experimentation many of these old stand-bys can be adapted and formatted for crockery-style cooking.

*The **basic rules** to follow are approximately these: 1 hour of conventional cooking needs to be replaced with 4 to 6 hours on low setting, or with about 2 to 3 ½ hours on the high setting of your slow cooker. Conventional-recipe liquids may need to be reduced by as much as 1/2 due to moisture retention in the slow-cooking process and seasonings may need to be adjusted from conventional recipes for prolonged-cooking satisfaction.*

So next time they ask "what's cookin'..." you just might reply with one of your Great Grandmother's recipes.

"Hand-Me-Down" Entrees Chapter Index

Papa Paul's BBQ'd Chicken

4-6 servings (depending on how hungry you are)

1 whole chicken, skinned and cut into serving-size pieces
Water
1 stalk celery, chunked
1 small onion, chunked
1/2 cup ketchup
1/4 cup water or broth
1/4 cup vinegar
1 teaspoon onion powder
1 tablespoon brown sugar
1-2 tablespoons soy sauce
Salt and pepper to taste

Place chicken in slow cooker with approximately 2 cups of water, the celery and the onion. Cook covered, on high setting for 4-6 hours (or low setting 6-8 hours). Remove chicken from slow cooker and temporarily set aside. Drain the pot and discard the water, celery and onion. Return the chicken to slow cooker. Make a BBQ sauce from the remaining ingredients (ketchup through salt and pepper) mixing well. Pour the sauce over the chicken and continue cooking (covered) on low setting for another 2 hours, or until chicken is very tender and sauce is well glazed over the chicken.

—*from the kitchen of Paul Tillman, adapted to crockery-style cooking by Wendy Louise*

Cook's Note: Serve with corn on the cob (see page 187) and other summer fare.

Family Favorite French Dip

8+ servings

1 (3 pound) beef roast (eye, rump or sirloin tip)
  Cook's Note: utilize your grocery store sale
1 large onion, sliced
2 cups beef broth
Water
6 pepper corns
1 bay leaf
Garlic cloves, smashed (use several, or to taste)
Salt and pepper to taste
1-2 loaves crusty French bread

Place sliced onion in slow cooker. Lay the roast on the onions. Pour the beef broth over the roast and add the spices. Add water until the roast is covered. Cover with lid and cook on high 5-6 hours, or low 10-12 hours, adding more water if necessary to keep the roast covered. Remove meat from slow cooker and let stand 5-10 minutes before slicing. Slice the meat across the grain. Set aside and keep warm. Strain the liquid (removing onion, pepper corns, garlic and bay leaf). Skim off any excess fat, making a nice 'dipping broth'. Return broth to slow cooker. Add meat slices back to slow  cooker to keep moist. (You can add more water or broth if necessary to make more 'au jus' for dipping.) Adjust seasonings with salt and pepper to taste. Serve the meat warm as sandwiches on French bread, with the dipping sauce provided in bowls on the side.

—adapted for crockery-style cooking from the kitchen of The Rush Hour Cook, Brook Noel

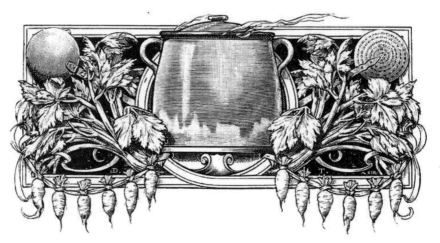

A Tip from the Kitchen...

A fun serving suggestion when using French bread for sandwiches, is to split the whole loaf down the middle, horizontally. Pile on the meat slices and close back up, making a giant sandwich. Let everyone slice off a portion-size to their liking and 'customize' their sandwich from a selection of condiments, you've provided on the side.

Super Sauce

2 pounds Italian sausage, crumbled

1 large onion, chopped

1 cup sliced mushrooms

4 cloves garlic, smashed and minced

2 (14.5 ounce) cans diced tomatoes, with liquid

1 (29 ounce) can tomato sauce

1 (12 ounce) can tomato paste

2 tablespoons dried basil

1 tablespoon sugar

1/2 teaspoon salt

½ teaspoon pepper

Brown sausage and onions with garlic (in batches) in a sauté pan. Transfer to slow cooker and add remaining ingredients (except mushrooms). Cover with lid and cook on high setting for 1 hour. Reduce to low setting and cook for 8-10 hours, or all day, or overnight. Sauté the mushrooms and add last hour of cooking.

Rush Hour Cook's Note: "Makes a ton! Save your emptied (and sterilized) commercial glass jars and fill with your homemade sauce. Freeze, leaving 'head room' of an inch for expansion. This can make a great quick gift. Prepare a pasta 'gift basket' with a jar or two of your homemade sauce, assorted noodles, a wedge of fresh Parmesan cheese and some pretty paper napkins and sturdy paper plates or bowls. Present in a decorative basket, including recipe instructions on a home-crafted card."

-from the kitchen of The Rush Hour Cook: Weekly Wonders ISBN 1891400142 by Brook Noel—Original recipe has been halved for crockery-style cooking.

Lucile's Smoked Pork Chops and Rice

4 servings

4 boneless, smoked pork chops (fully cooked)
2 ½ cups chicken broth
1 ½ cups long grain rice, uncooked
1 medium onion, diced
1 teaspoon dried parsley flakes, crumbled between fingers
1 pinch of dried oregano, crumbled between fingers
1 (10 3/4 ounce) can cream of celery soup (undiluted)
1 shot of Worcestershire sauce
Minced garlic (optional)
Black pepper to taste

Set pork chops aside. Mix the rest of the ingredients together and place half of the mixture into the slow cooker. Next, arrange the smoked pork chops into the slow cooker, forming a middle layer. Top with the remaining rice mixture. Cover with lid and cook on high for 3-4 hours, 'til rice is plumped and tender. Adjust seasoning if necessary, baring in mind that the smoked pork chops provide the salt needed for this recipe.

Cook's Note: Serve with a refreshing fruit salad of canned peach or pear halves, nestled in lettuce leaves. Top each fruit half with a dollop of cottage cheese, or a wedge of cream cheese, or a spoonful of whipped fruit-flavored cream cheese for an instant salad.

—from the kitchen of Lucile Feiereisen, adapted for crockery-style cooking by Wendy Louise

A Tip from the Kitchen...

When in doubt, we all serve a simply-tossed salad at the drop of a hat. Don't forget about the refreshing change of pace that fresh fruit can bring to the table. The addition of mandarin orange slices, grapefruit sections or fresh pineapple can add interest to your everyday-tossed salad. A sliced fresh peach or kiwi can be used as well, pairing nicely with your favorite vinaigrette over mixed greens. Be creative and you might get your kids to add salad to their menu.

Mom' Pork Chops with Scalloped Potatoes

Cook's Note: This dish smells divine while cooking.

Allow 1 pork chop (bone in) per person
Allow 1 large potato per person, plus a couple extra for good
  luck
Milk
Oregano, crushed to release flavor
Salt and pepper to taste
Butter
Flour

Thinly slice the potatoes and place into slow cooker. Salt and pepper to taste. Sprinkle a little flour over the top of the potatoes and dot with butter. Arrange the pork chops on top of the potatoes. Pour milk over the chops and potatoes, to a depth of halfway up the potatoes. Sprinkle with oregano to taste. Cover and simmer on low setting, until pork chops are thoroughly cooked and the potatoes are "scalloped" to fork tender (at least 6 hours). If cooked on high you can reduce the cooking time to approximately 4 hours.

—from the kitchen of Betty Tillman, adapted for crockery-style cooking by Wendy Louise

A Tip from the Kitchen...

You will notice in these hand-me-down recipes that measurement, precision and exactitude are beginning to fall by the wayside. A "casualness" is taking over as the recipes become more descriptive than directive... We are talking Grandmother...and Mother... and Mother-in-Laws' Language now.—They measured with a hollow palm, a dollop, a dab, a pat, a package, a peck, a lug... and a pinch for good measure.

Mom's Stuffed Flank Steak

4-6 servings

1 flank steak, the largest you can find
1 package seasoned stuffing-style bread cubes, such as
    Pepperidge Farm® (or make your own with about 4
    slices of day-old bread cut into cubes, sprinkled with
    seasonings of choice and sautéed in a little butter and
    minced onion for flavor.)
Cooking oil
1/2 cup water or broth

Score the flank steak with a sharp knife, making a diagonal
pattern of slashes across the grain. Put the stuffing down
the center of the steak and roll up jelly-roll fashion, with the
scored side facing out. Secure with toothpicks. Brown the
steak on all sides in a little oil. Transfer to a slow cooker
sprayed with cooking spray and add 1/2 cup water or broth.
Cover with lid and cook on low setting 6-9 hours, or on high
setting 3 ½ -5 hours. During cooking add small amounts of
broth or water if necessary. To serve, remove toothpicks
and cut into 1/2-inch thick slices. Arrange slices on platter
and drizzle with gravy made from the cooking juices. Let
each person salt and pepper their serving to taste.

*—from the kitchen of Betty Tillman, adapted for crockery-style cooking by
Wendy Louise*

Cook's Note: A tougher cut of meat, flank steak used to
be extremely inexpensive...until people discovered how
truly delicious it could be. Since there are only two flank
cuts per steer, it has become a rather expensive cut of meat,
in today's market.

A Tip from the Kitchen...

For a spicier version of this same recipe, marinate the scored steak in Italian or Russian-style salad dressing before stuffing. Remove steak from marinade and discard excess marinade; stuff the steak and proceed per recipe instructions.

Caleb's Brat's 'N Beer

At least 2 brat sausages per person
A corresponding amount of good buns
Beer
Water (optional)
Whole pepper corns
Red pepper flakes

Variation # 1

Pierce brats with fork and place in slow cooker. Pour on beer (and water) to cover. Add seasonings, cover with lid and precook brats on high setting until plumped, juicy and fully cooked (about 4 hours on high, or all day on low). Timing isn't really critical. Go off to water ski or play your guitar. When you return finish the brats on the grill, browning nicely. Serve on buns along with corn on the cob (see page 187)

Variation # 2

If it's raining pierce the sausages with fork (so they don't blow up) and brown on all sides in a skillet. Place in slow cooker with the beer and seasonings, and finish cooking that way. Hold on low setting until ready to serve.

Recipe submitted by Rob Bensen, Friend, Humorist and Self-taught Chef

A Tip from the Kitchen...
An advantage to cooking with a slow cooker in the summertime is that it takes both the heat and the cook out of the kitchen!

Mom's Easy Old Fashioned Meat and Potatoes

6-8 servings

1 (3 pound) beef roast
Water
1 packet French onion soup mix for seasoning

Place roast in slow cooker. Sprinkle with seasoning packet. Add a splash of water (about 1 cup). Cover with lid and cook on low setting all day.

Cook's Note: Serve with homemade mashed potatoes and gravy made from the crockery-juices. Vegetables optional. Salad optional. Side dishes optional.

A "Meat and Potatoes Guy" —recipe submitted by Craig Heun, Champion Press Ltd. Shipping Department Coordinator, Song writer and Musician.

The Rush Hour Cook's Pot Roast Perfection

10-12 servings

1 (3 pound) beef roast
1 pound onions, sliced
1/8 cup water
1 (12 ounce) bottle of beer
1 cup water
1 package oxtail soup mix

In a large pan mix 1/8 cup water with onions and stir for 5 minutes. Transfer onions to slow cooker. Add beer, soup mix and 1 cup water to slow cooker and stir well. Place meat into mixture. Cover with lid and cook on low setting for 6-8 hours, or until very tender. Let stand 10 minutes before serving.

Cook's Note: Although the beer is absorbed in this recipe you can substitute beef broth in its place, if you like.

Excerpted from The Rush Hour Cook: Weekly Wonders ISBN 1891400142 by Brook Noel

Julie's "Ring-the-dinner-bell" Bell Peppers

8 servings

8 large bell peppers (green, yellow or red)
1-1 ½ pounds ground beef
1 onion, diced
2 large tomatoes, diced
2 tablespoons vinegar
1 teaspoon sugar
1 teaspoon cinnamon
1/4 teaspoon cumin
1 teaspoon sea salt
1/2 cup raisins (plumped and drained)
Green chilies or chili powder, to taste
1/2 cup slivered almonds, or pine nuts (optional)

Cap the peppers and hollow out ribs and seeds. Set aside. To make filling sauté the ground beef and onion until onion is transparent and meat is browned. Drain off any excess fat. Add the rest of the ingredients (except the nuts) and mix well. Gently pack filling into peppers. Carefully place filled peppers, side by side, down into a well greased slow cooker. Pile any extra filling on top of all, if necessary. Cover with lid and cook on low for 4-6 hours, or until peppers are tender (but not mushy) and filling is set. Garnish with slivered almonds or pine nuts just before serving. (See *A Tip from the Kitchen*, page 198.)

—*Caleb and Julies' Tuesday night dinner, submitted by Wendy Louise*

Mary's Special Meat Balls

6-8 servings

4 pounds ground beef
Minced onion, to taste
Minced garlic, to taste
Salt and pepper, to taste
1 cup apple sauce
2 cups crushed cornflakes
2 eggs, beaten

Toss all gently to mix and form into large meat balls. Sauté in a little oil to gently brown on all sides. Transfer meatballs to slow cooker.

1 stick butter
1 medium onion, diced
1/3 cup flour
4 cups beef broth
1 bottle chili sauce
2/3 cup tomato paste
Garlic, crushed basil and cracked pepper to taste
2 tablespoons beef concentrate
1 tablespoon Worcestershire sauce
1/2 cup red wine or water
Sliced fresh mushrooms

Make a roux with the butter, onion and flour. Incorporate the remaining ingredients (except for the mushrooms) and simmer to blend into a sauce. Pour the sauce over the meatballs in the slow cooker. Cover with lid and cook on low setting for 6-8 hours, or on high setting for 3-5 hours. Sauté the fresh mushrooms in a little butter and add to slow cooker during last 1/2 hour of cooking. Serve over buttered noodles.

—from the kitchen of Mary Propernick, adapted for crockery-style cooking by Wendy Louise

A Tip from the Kitchen...

Cooking with the addition of wine, whisky, sherry, and beer can add special flavor to your recipe and help tenderize the meat. It should be noted, however, that any of these may be replaced with water, broth, tea or fruit juice if you prefer.

Betty's Lamb with Burgundy Sauce

6 servings

6 lamb (shoulder-cut) chops
A little butter or oil
1 large onion, sliced into rings
Water
1 package carrots, cut into chunks
1 cup Burgundy wine
Beef broth or beef bouillon
Flour and water (to thicken gravy)
Salt and pepper to taste

Brown the shoulder chops on each side in a little butter or oil, adding the onions to the pan for a few minutes to glaze in pan juices. Transfer chops and onions to slow cooker. Add water just to cover chops. Add carrots and wine. Cover and simmer on low-heat setting for 6-8 hours. Add beef broth or bouillon and continue simmering for another hour, or until chops are fork tender. Turn slow cooker setting to high. In a separate dish, blend together a little flour and water to make a smooth thickening agent. Slowly blend the mixture into the crockery-juices to thicken your gravy, stirring until incorporated. Simmer, uncovered on high setting, until gravy thickens to your liking. Adjust your gravy with salt and pepper to taste. **Cook's Note:** Serve with mashed potatoes and/or crusty French bread.

—from the kitchen of Betty Tillman, adapted for crockery-style cooking by Wendy Louise

A Tip from the Kitchen...

Many of these heirloom recipes do not have exact measurements. As I mentioned before, our mothers used to cook with a little bit of this and a little bit of that. If something wasn't available, they just substituted something else. Somehow their meals always turned out creatively delicious; and if we 'cleaned our plates' we were rewarded with a fabulous dessert. (So clean up your plate! and check out our dessert section on pages 210 through 230.)

Mother's Garden Stew
(served with dumplings, spatzen or spatzle)
6 servings

Round steak, cut into 6 generous 1/2-inch thick slices
Flour
Butter
Salt and pepper
Oregano, crushed between fingers
Garlic powder
Water as needed
Fresh green beans (preferably picked from the garden),
    cleaned and de-veined, ends and tips snipped off
Cooking sherry or port (optional)

Brown round steak slices (that have been dusted with flour) in a little butter. While browning, season the meat with salt, pepper, oregano and garlic powder to taste. Transfer the slices to a slow cooker and add a little water. Cover. Cook on high heat setting till meat is very tender (approximately 2-4 hours). Add water as necessary. During the last half hour of cooking add 6 handfuls of freshly-picked and cleaned garden- green beans. Add a dash of cooking sherry or port to taste (optional). Cover. Continue to cook on high setting until beans are tender/crisp/chewy. During the last 15 minutes of cooking add your old fashioned dumplings (see recipe on following page), cover and continue to cook until dumplings are done (shiny and set).

Old Fashioned Dumplings

2 cups flour
4 teaspoons baking powder
1/2 teaspoon salt
1 pinch of crushed oregano
1 cup milk

Mix all into a blended batter, taking care to not over-mix! Drop by teaspoonfuls onto the cooking stew. Cover and continue cooking on high setting. Cook until dumplings are shiny and set. The dumplings will automatically thicken the stew, forming nice gravy.

Cook's Note: You can cook your dumplings separately, in a pot of boiling water. They will automatically float to the top when done. This takes approximately 10 to 15 minutes. They make a delicious addition to soups and other stews found in this book, or simply served as a side dish, drizzled with melted butter.

—from the kitchen of Lucile Feiereisen, adapted for crockery-style cooking by Wendy Louise

A Tip from the Kitchen...

When cooking dumplings in a slow cooker take care to make them small, dropping by teaspoonfuls rather than tablespoonfuls for quicker and more even cooking.

Lucile's Spatzen

4 servings

1 egg, well beaten
1/2 teaspoon salt
1/3 cup water
3/4 cup flour
Melted butter

Mix all ingredients, except melted butter, together to form a smooth, soft dough. Drop by small teaspoonfuls into a kettle of boiling water. Cook approximately 10 minutes, covered. Drain in colander and toss with melted butter. Serve these mini dumplings as a side dish for stews and meat-with-gravy dishes, in place of potatoes.

Lucile's Spatzle

4 servings

Fold 1 tablespoon oil into the above dough and blend smooth. Force the dough through the holes of a colander into the boiling liquid. Or form the dough into a patty shape (on waxed paper or oiled surface) and slice off noodle-shaped-slivers and slide into boiling liquid. These mini-mini noodles only need about 5 minutes to cook. Toss with melted butter and serve as above.

—from the kitchen of Lucile Feiereisen

Hunter's Delight

6 servings

2 ½ pounds ground beef
1 large onion, chopped
Salt and pepper to taste
6 large potatoes, sliced
2 cans whole kernel corn, drained
1 can cream of mushroom soup
1 (soup can) milk
1 small can mushrooms, drained
1 diced green pepper

In a frying pan brown the ground beef. When almost brown drain and put into slow cooker. Add onion, potatoes, corn, mushrooms and green pepper to slow cooker. Mix in cream of mushroom soup and milk, stirring to blend. Cover with lid and cook on low setting for 3 hours.

—from the kitchen of Glenn Koopmann

A Really Good German Pot Roast

8 servings

Cook's Note: This recipe requires some overnight preparation and all-day cooking the next day

1 (4 pound) beef brisket, trim off the fat and reserve
2 teaspoons McCormick's Season-All®
1 teaspoon ground ginger
1 garlic clove, smashed
1/2 teaspoon dry mustard
2 cups red wine vinegar
1 cup water
2 onions, quartered
2 bay leaves
2 teaspoons mixed pickling spices
1 teaspoon whole black peppercorns
8 whole cloves
1/2 cup sugar
2 teaspoons vegetable oil
6 ginger snaps, crushed

Rub meat with Season-All®, ginger and garlic clove. Place in large bowl. In a saucepan combine remaining ingredients, except trimmed fat and ginger snaps. Bring to a boil and pour over meat. Cool, cover tightly and place in refrigerator overnight to marinate. Remove meat and save the marinade. Pat the roast dry with a paper towel. Heat the fat in a heavy skillet until it is sizzling. Carefully sear the roast on all sides. Place in slow cooker . Pour the reserved marinade over the roast. Cover with lid and cook on low setting for 8-10 hours, or until meat is fork tender. Remove roast to serving platter and slice. Serve with spatzle or buttered noodles and gravy made from the cooking juices.

Recipe contributed by Michael Gulan, Publishing Assistant

The Rush Hour Cook's Quick-to-Mix, Long-to-Cook Italian Roast

8 servings

1 (3 pound) beef round roast
1 onion, sliced
2 garlic cloves, minced
1/2 teaspoon salt
1/2 teaspoon pepper
1 (8 ounce) can tomato sauce
1 package Italian salad dressing mix

Place sliced onion in bottom of slow cooker. Add roast. Top with remaining ingredients. Cover with lid and cook on high setting for 5 hours, or until meat is fork tender. Slice or shred and serve on Kaiser Rolls.

Excerpted from The Rush Hour Cook presents Effortless Entertaining ISBN 189140086X By Brook Noel

A Tip from the Kitchen...

For a party, try serving this recipe submarine-sandwich-style as suggested in the kitchen tip on page 102. Arrange your sandwich on a decorative platter, surrounded by colorful condiments. Make it the **edible** centerpiece of your table!

June's Famous Beef Brisket

6-8 servings

1 (3 ½ pound) beef brisket, have the butcher select you a
   nice one
1 large onion, chunked
1 can of beer
1/2 cup chili sauce
2 tablespoons brown sugar
Salt and pepper to taste

Place brisket in slow cooker, fat side down. Surround the roast with onion chunks. Mix the beer, chili sauce, brown sugar and seasonings; and pour over the roast. Cover with lid and cook on high setting for 1 hour. Reduce setting to low and cook for 10-12 hours more, until meat is very tender. Remove meat and let sit for 10 minutes. Slice the meat on the bias, across the grain for tender slices. Or shred meat if desired. De-fat the cooking juices left in the slow cooker and return the meat to the pot to moisten. Serve warm as sandwiches, or as a main course with a side of mashed potatoes.

Cook's Note: The meat may be stored in its juices to be kept moist; refrigerate or freeze.

—from the kitchen of June Kirzan, Writer, Story Teller, and darn good cook

Author's Note: There is this charming lady who lives in my apartment complex, who has happened to have taken me under her wing. Her name is June. Whenever she makes her wonderful brisket she leaves a succulent sandwich on my stoop. When I arrive home from work, there it is, packed in its little Tupperware® container...just for me. Yum! There is this charming lady...her name is June...

Author's Note continued: If any one could rival June in a Brisket Contest it would be Donna (even though she uses sirloin tip). Her recipe (on the following page) is perhaps my favorite in the book due to its absolute ease and tasty results. There is this woman...her name is Donna...and can she cook!

Donna's Italian Beef for Sandwiches

8-10 servings

1 (3 pound) sirloin tip roast
1 jar of mild Italian giardiniera-style vegetables (found in the condiment or specialized food section of your grocery store) un-drained

Place sirloin tip roast in slow cooker, fat side down with butcher strings removed. Pour the jar of vegetables, with oil and juices, over the roast. Cover with lid and cook on high setting for 1 hour. Reduce to low setting and cook for 10-12 hours more, or until meat is extremely tender. Carefully remove meat from slow cooker, de-fat the juices, and return the meat to the slow cooker. Stir with a fork; the meat will automatically shred.

Cook's Note: Serve the meat on open-faced sandwiches of toasted garlic bread, meat piled high and mozzarella cheese melted over the top. (Put sandwiches under broiler just long enough to melt the cheese.) If you start the meat in your slow cooker the night before, it will be ready for sandwiches by noon the next day.

—*from the kitchen of Donna Wood, "Woods-woman Extraordinaire"*

Tuscan-Style Pork Roast

8-12 servings

1 (3 pound) pork loin, on the bone
2 tablespoons olive oil
1/2 teaspoon pepper
1/2 cup dry white wine
4 garlic cloves, halved
1 tablespoon rosemary
1/2 teaspoon salt

Make small slits in the roast and insert garlic slivers (see *Kitchen Tip* for infusing garlic, page 94). In a small bowl mix the oil, rosemary, pepper and salt. Rub the roast with the seasoning mixture and place in the slow cooker. Pour 1/2 cup wine over the roast Cover with lid and cook on low setting 8-10 hours, or until meat is incredibly tender.

Excerpted and adapted from The Rush Hour Cook: Weekly Wonders ISBN 1891400142 by Brook Noel

A Tip from the Kitchen...

Garlic may be easily peeled by removing individual cloves from the head and smashing under the broad side of the blade of a chef's knife. The garlic will 'smoosh' right out of the peel, as you put pressure on the side of the blade with the heel of your hand.

Mom's Easy as 1-2-3 Pork Roast

6-8 servings

1 (2-3 pound) pork loin
1/2 cup water
1 package dry onion soup mix

Rub seasonings from soup packet over the roast and place in slow cooker. Add the water. Cover with lid and cook all day on low setting.

Cook's Note: Make gravy from the roasting juices and serve with mashed potatoes.

-Recipe submitted by that "Meat and Potatoes Guy", Craig Heun, Champion Press Ltd. Shipping Department Coordinator, Linguist and Impersonator

Balsamic-Spice Marinade for Pork Roast

1 teaspoon sugar
1 teaspoon ground pepper
1/2 teaspoon salt
1/2 teaspoon coriander
1/2 teaspoon ground ginger
1-2 tablespoons olive oil
1 tablespoon balsamic vinegar

Mix all together and rub over roast to coat all sides. Wrap in plastic wrap and marinate meat in refrigerator overnight before cooking in your favorite recipe.

Excerpted from Cooking for Blondes, gourmet recipes for the culinarily challenged ISBN 1891400940 by Rhonda Levitch

Mom's Easy Marinade

1 packet of Four Seasons® Italian Salad Dressing
5 mashed garlic cloves
Freshly cracked pepper

Mix salad dressing according to package directions, in your special bottle just for marinade. Add some smashed garlic cloves and freshly cracked pepper. Pour over meat and marinate in a glass dish in refrigerator, turning once in a while.

-from the kitchen of Betty Tillman

Mom's Magic Seasoning

Mix any and all "dibs and dabs" from your almost empty spice bottles together. Keep in a cute little crock or jar on the stove and add a pinch to your cooking when the spirit moves you.

-from the kitchen of Betty Tillman

Grandma's Three Bean Hot Dish

6 servings

2 cans pork and beans
2 cans butter beans, drained
1 cup brown sugar
1 cup sugar
2 cans red kidney beans, drained
1 cup ketchup
1/4 cup honey
1 ½ pounds bacon, cut and fried
1 pound ground beef, browned
1 ½ cup chopped onion
Salt and pepper to taste

Mix all ingredients together in slow cooker. Cover with lid and cook on low heat for 3-4 hours. (Unlike Grandma) go surf the net and come back when it's done.

Recipe contributed by MaryAnn Koopmann, Career Woman and Homemaker

---

Sara's Lovely Little Links Casserole

8 servings

2 packages Little Smokies®-style sausages
1 (16 ounce) bag of frozen peas
8 potatoes, sliced
1 can cream of mushroom soup
1 can cream of celery soup
1 onion, chopped

Place ingredients in this order in the slow cooker: Onions, potatoes, sausages, peas and both soups. Cover with lid and cook on low for 6-8 hours.

—from the kitchen of Sara Pattow

Chapter Four:
Dinner is Served...
Fancier Entrees

"Dinner is served..." Bring out the china, press the napkins and light the candles, these recipes are for special dinners when you want to entertain with creativity and flair. Or maybe you are having a formal family night with an un-hurried dinner and catch-up conversation. We all appreciate a change of pace now and then, and a relaxed dinner with fancier fare just might be the answer.

Fancier Entrees Chapter Index

Bacon-Wrapped Chicken Breasts

4 servings

4 boneless skinless chicken breasts (can be thawed or
   frozen)
8 slices thick smoked bacon
1 jar of your favorite barbecue sauce
1 shot of whisky (preferably Jack Daniels)
1 tablespoon hot sauce

Wrap chicken breasts with 2 bacon strips each. Set aside.
Pour barbecue sauce, whisky and hot sauce into slow
cooker. Place wrapped chicken breasts in pot and cover
with lid. Cook on low setting for 6-8 hours.

Cook's Note: Serve on buns, or with crusty bread and a
broccoli side dish, or with your favorite potato dish.

—from the kitchen of "Miz Malibu"

Chicken Tango

6-8 servings

1 whole chicken, cut up, skin removed
1 extra chicken breast, skin removed, cut in half
1 bottle of Russian fat-free salad dressing
1 small jar apricot preserves
1 teaspoon salt
1/4 teaspoon pepper
1 cup water, boiling

Place chicken in slow cooker. Pour the Russian salad dressing over each piece. Combine boiling water with the apricot jam. Add the salt and pepper and mix well, then pour the thinned preserves over the chicken. Cover with lid and cook on low setting for 7-9 hours.

Excerpted from Crazy About Crockery! 101 Recipes for Entertaining at less than .75 cents a serving ISBN 1891400525 by Penny E. Stone

South African Chicken

6 servings

Cook's Note: This recipe requires overnight marinating.

6 onions, sliced thin
6 cloves garlic, pressed
1/4 cup lemon juice
Salt and pepper to taste
1 (3-4 pound) chicken, cut up into serving pieces
1 tablespoon olive oil

In a large zipper-type bag, combine onions, garlic, lemon juice, salt and pepper. Add chicken pieces and zip up the bag. Roll the chicken around in the bag to coat. Refrigerate over night to marinate. Remove chicken from the marinade and pour the marinade into the slow cooker. In a skillet over medium-high heat, brown the chicken pieces in a little olive oil. Transfer chicken to slow cooker, putting the dark meat pieces on the bottom, white meat on top. Cover with lid and cook on low setting for 4-6 hours, or until chicken is thoroughly done. When chicken is done, remove from slow cooker and reserve, keeping warm. Transfer the remaining cooking juices and onions into a skillet and cook for about 10 minutes, or until reduced by half. Serve the chicken with brown rice and spoon the reduced sauce over everything.

Excerpted from The Frantic Family Cookbook (mostly) healthy meals in minutes ISBN 1189400118 by Leanne Ely, C.N.C.

A Tip from the Kitchen...

Turn off the TV—Turn on the stereo—Feed all your senses.
Accompany your meal with soft dinner music. People will
linger longer, talk longer and eat slower. If you are having a
'theme dinner' choose coordinating music.

Chinese Crockery Chicken

8 servings

1 whole chicken (about 3 pounds)
1/4 cup soy sauce
1/4 cup orange marmalade
2 tablespoons ketchup
6 cloves garlic, pressed
1 onion, sliced
Salt and pepper to taste

Place your chicken in the slow cooker. Mix together soy sauce, marmalade and ketchup, and pour over the chicken. Then add garlic and onions, a teeny bit of salt (won't need much because of the soy sauce) and pepper. Cover with lid and cook on low setting for about 10-12 hours. Chicken should be falling off the bone when ready. Serve with rice.

Excerpted from Healthy Foods, an irreverent guide to understanding nutrition and feeding your family well ISBN 1891400207 by Leanne Ely, C.N.C.

A Tip from the Kitchen...

Cooking on high setting generally cuts your cooking time in half. Want to get your dish done in an afternoon?—Set your slow cooker on high. Going off to work? Spending a day with the girls?—Set your slow cooker on low and let it simmer all day.

Company's Coming to Dinner Chicken

6-8 servings

1 whole chicken, washed and cleaned and patted dry
Butter
1 medium onion, coarsely chopped
Several cloves of garlic, peeled and smashed
Baby new potatoes, scrubbed and peeled around
  their centers (rest of skin left on)
2 carrots, chunked
2 ribs of celery, chunked
1 lemon, juice and rind
1/4 cup cooking vermouth
1/4 cup chicken broth
Salt and pepper to taste
Paprika (optional)

In bottom of slow cooker arrange onion, garlic, new potatoes, carrots and celery. Nestle the whole chicken (breast up) down into the pot, resting on the vegetables. Dot the cavity with butter. Halve or quarter lemon and squeeze juice over all. Immerse the left-over rinds down into the vegetables. Drizzle the vermouth and chicken broth over all. Salt and pepper to taste. Sprinkle the chicken with a dusting of paprika (for color). Cover with lid and cook on low setting for at least 8-10 hours, or until chicken is literally falling from the bone. Add additional vermouth or broth if necessary.

Cook's Note: To serve, carefully remove the whole chicken to a deep dish platter and surround with a border of the cooked vegetables and their juices, discarding the lemon rinds. Add a loaf of crusty French bread and a nice salad, and you have it made! Enjoy!

—Originally cooked in a clay pot, adapted for slow cooker-style cooking from the kitchen of Wendy Louise

Chicken Parisian
6 servings

6 medium chicken breasts
Salt and pepper
Paprika
1/2 cup dry white wine or vermouth or broth
1 (10.5 ounce) can condensed cream of mushroom soup
1 (4 ounce) can sliced mushrooms, drained
1 cup dairy sour cream, mixed with
 1/4 cup flour (be sure to see **Cook's Note** below)

Sprinkle chicken breasts lightly with salt, pepper and paprika. Place into slow cooker. Mix together the white wine, soup, mushrooms, and the flour-thickened sour cream. Pour over chicken breasts in slow cooker. Sprinkle with additional paprika. Cover with lid and cook on low setting 6-8 hours. Serve chicken and sauce over rice or noodles.

Cook's Note: If you elect to cook this dish on high setting, for 2 ½ -3 ½ hours, you must add the thickened sour cream during the last 30 minutes of cooking, to minimize the chances of your sauce separating. *—from the kitchen of Joan Egan*

A Tip from the Kitchen...

Get out the linen napkins... Have your kids set the table and fold the napkins into fancy folds and place in the center of each plate. (There are even books on napkin folding!) Or flare the napkins out of long stemmed glasses. Put a pitcher of ice water, flavored with lemon slices, on the table. Kids love to drink out of "special glasses" and you'll add to your daily water quotient as well!

Chicken Mushroom Supreme

6 servings

1 whole chicken, cut up, skin removed

2 cups water

2 stalks celery, broken into 3-4 -inch pieces

2 medium onions, chop one and leave the other whole

1 teaspoon salt

2 ¼ cups uncooked instant rice

2 cans cream of mushroom soup

1 can cream of celery soup

1 cup water

2 small cans of mushroom pieces, drained

1 cup dried bread crumbs

3 tablespoons butter

1 additional teaspoon salt

1/4 teaspoon pepper

Place skinless chicken pieces in slow cooker. Add 2 cups water, 2 stalks celery cut into 3-4 -inch pieces, the whole onion, and a teaspoon of salt. Cover with lid  and cook on high setting for 6 hours. Remove meat from slow cooker and empty all vegetables and broth. (Can strain and save the broth for another recipe.) Let meat cool then pick off the bones and return small pieces of chicken back to the slow cooker. Add soups, 1 cup water, drained mushrooms, uncooked instant rice, medium chopped onion, dried bread crumbs, butter and additional teaspoon of salt and the pepper. Stir to mix well. Cover with lid and cook on high setting for 3 more hours.

Excerpted from Crazy About Crockery! 101 Easy and Inexpensive Recipes for Less than .75 cents a serving ISBN 1891400126 by Penny E. Stone

Chicken Broccoli Divan

6 servings

1 whole chicken, cut up, skin removed
3 cups water
1 teaspoon salt
2 packages frozen broccoli, thawed
2 cans cream of chicken soup
1 teaspoon lemon juice
1/2 cup mayonnaise
1/2 teaspoon curry powder
1/2 cup dried bread crumbs
1 cup shredded Cheddar cheese
3 tablespoons butter, melted

Place chicken pieces in slow cooker with water and 1 teaspoon salt. Cover with lid and cook on high setting for 6 hours. Carefully remove chicken from slow cooker and set aside to cool. Discard broth (or save for another recipe). Place thawed broccoli in bottom of emptied slow cooker. Pick the chicken off the bone and tear into bite-sized pieces. Add chicken back over broccoli. In separate bowl, combine soup, lemon juice, mayonnaise, curry powder and melted butter, mixing well. Pour soup mixture over chicken. Top with bread crumbs and Cheddar cheese. Cover with lid and continue cooking on high for 2-4 hours. Serve with a tossed salad (see suggestions in *Kitchen Tip*, page 105.)

Excerpted from Crazy About Crockery! 101 Easy and Inexpensive Recipes for Less than .75 cents a serving ISBN 1891400126 by Penny E. Stone

Chicken with Champagne and Cream

6 servings

6 boneless, skinless chicken breast halves
1 teaspoon thyme, crushed between fingers
Salt and white pepper to taste
1 stick butter
1 cup champagne
1 tablespoon flour
1 ½ cups heavy whipping cream
Optional garnish (portabella mushroom slice and chive
  sprigs)

Season the chicken breasts with thyme, salt and pepper and then sauté lightly in the butter. Transfer the sautéed chicken to slow cooker. In the sauté pan, add the flour to the sauté butter, stirring to make a roux. Then stir in the champagne and cook till sauce thickens. Pour sauce over chicken in slow cooker. Cover with lid and cook on low setting for 3-4 hours, or until chicken is very tender. Remove chicken from slow cooker and keep warm on a heated platter. Turn heat setting to low and stir the heavy cream into slow cooker to 'finish' your sauce. Cook only until sauce is heated through. Swirl in 1 tablespoon of butter (optional). Pour sauce over chicken and serve.

—*from the kitchen of Betty Tillman, adapted for crockery-style cooking by Wendy Louise*

(continued next page...)

Cook's Note: Garnish each serving with a large slice of sautéed portabella mushroom and sprigs of fresh chive for that extra touch.

A Tip from the Kitchen...

If you find your sauces or gravies are coming out too thin, uncover the slow cooker and cook for 15 minutes on high setting to reduce the liquid and 'finish' the sauce. Color not right? —add some Kitchen Bouquet®, Sauce Robert® or paprika. Enrich your sauce by swirling in one tablespoon of butter at the very end —(it's a French thing.)

Beef in Wine Sauce
4-6 servings

2 pounds stew meat, cut into 1-inch pieces
1 envelope onion-soup mix
1 (10.5 ounce) can cream of mushroom soup
1 (4 ounce) can whole button mushrooms
1/2 cup dry red or cooking wine, port or sherry (your
    choice)

Combine all ingredients in slow cooker, mixing together well. Cover with lid and cook on low setting for 8-12 hours. Serve over a rice pilaf or buttered noodles along with crusty French bread and a glass of wine.

—from the kitchen of Lucile Feiereisen, adapted for crockery-style cooking by Wendy Louise

Beef Burgundy
6-8 servings

2-4 pounds beef round steak, trimmed of all fat
1 cup Burgundy wine
1 medium onion, finely chopped
1 large clove of garlic, crushed
1 can cream of mushroom soup
1 cup water
1 package dry onion soup mix
1 can whole mushrooms, drained
1 bay leaf
1 tablespoon parsley flakes

Trim meat of all fat and cut into bite-sized pieces. Place in slow cooker. Mix the rest of the ingredients (except for parsley and bay leaf) together until well blended and pour over meat. Toss to coat well. Sprinkle with parsley and add the bay leaf. Cover with lid and simmer on low 8-10 hours, or until meat is fork tender. Adjust seasonings with salt and pepper to taste, if necessary. Remove bay leaf. Serve with buttered noodles and a nice salad.

Excerpted and adapted from 365 Quick, Easy and Inexpensive Dinner Menus ISBN 1891400339 by Penny E. Stone

A Tip from the Kitchen...
When using lighted candles at the dinner table, choose unscented ones. You don't want the scent of the candle to over power or conflict with the taste and aroma of your dinner.

Dorothea's French Style Meat Loaf

6-8 servings

1 pound ground beef
1 pound ground ham
1 large onion, finely chopped
1/2 cup raisins (soaked, plumped and drained)
1 cup dry bread crumbs
2 tablespoons cognac or brandy
2 eggs, separated
2 tablespoons butter
1/2 teaspoon freshly grated nutmeg
Salt and pepper to taste

Gently mix the first 6 ingredients thoroughly, then add the egg yolks and seasonings, mixing again. Beat the egg whites stiff and fold into the meat mixture. Form into a loaf and place in a buttered (or non-stick sprayed) slow cooker. Dot top of loaf with 2 tablespoons butter. Cover with lid and cook on low setting for 8-10 hours, or high setting 4-5 hours. Serve with parsley buttered new potatoes and a nice vegetable.

—Original recipe from the kitchen of Dorothea Loescher, a true lady of grace, adapted for crockery-style cooking by Wendy Louise

A Tip from the Kitchen...

Separating your eggs and beating the whites stiff, before folding into a meat loaf makes for a lighter, more delicate loaf.

Beef and Olives

6 servings

3-4 pounds chuck roast, trimmed of excess fat
1 onion, sliced
1 cup salad olives, with juice
Salt and pepper to taste
2 tablespoons Worcestershire sauce

Place meat in slow cooker and cover with onion slices. Combine remaining ingredients and pour over meat and onions. Cover with lid and cook on high setting for 6-8 hours.

Excerpted from Crazy About Crockery! 101 Easy and Inexpensive Recipes for Less than .75 cents a serving ISBN 1891400126 by Penny E. Stone

Ginger Beef with Broccoli
8 servings

2-5 pounds lean round steak, cut into serving portions
4-6 slices fresh ginger root
2 tablespoons soy sauce
1 teaspoon salt
12 green onions, chopped (including tops)
2 bunches fresh broccoli, cut into spears
2 teaspoons cornstarch
1 cup cold water
2 teaspoons Kitchen Bouquet® (browning and flavoring
   sauce)

Place pieces of meat in slow cooker. Add ginger root and green onions over meat. Drizzle soy sauce over meat. Dissolve the cornstarch in the cup of cold water and stir in the Kitchen Bouquet®. Pour over contents in slow cooker. Cover with lid and cook on high setting for 4 hours. Add broccoli to slow cooker. Sprinkle with salt. Cover again with lid and cook on low setting for another 3 hours.

Excerpted from Crazy About Crockery! 101 Recipes for Entertaining at less than .75 cents a serving 1891400525 by Penny E. Stone

Pepper Steak
served with Rice

6 servings

2-3 pounds round steak, cut into strips
1 cup water
1-2 cloves garlic, smashed and minced
1 tablespoon cornstarch
2 tablespoons butter, melted
2 tablespoons soy sauce
2 beef bouillon cubes, or equivalent in granules
1 large green bell pepper, cut into strips
1 onion, rustically cut
1/4 teaspoon coarsely ground black pepper
Thinly sliced water chestnuts (optional)

Combine melted butter and water in slow cooker. Stir in minced garlic, cornstarch, soy sauce, black pepper and beef bouillon cubes (or granules) until dissolved. Add the green pepper and onion strips. Cut meat into thin strips about 2-inches long by 1/4-inch wide (kind of 'stir fry' size). Add meat to slow cooker. Cover with lid and let cook for 6-8 hours on low setting. Last half hour stir in sliced water chestnuts for contrasting texture. At end of cooking adjust seasonings if necessary. Serve over cooked rice.

—*from the kitchen of Betty Tillman*

A Tip from the Kitchen...

When cutting vegetables and meats for slow-cooking cut them to uniform size to ensure even cooking. If cutting beforehand and storing in fridge, always store **raw** meats separate from vegetables until ready to use. If marinating the meat use a glass dish (rather than metal) or a plastic bag to avoid acidic interactions between the marinade and the container.

Pork Roast with Sweet Potatoes

6 servings

3-4 pound pork roast, trimmed of fat

3-4 sweet potatoes or yams, peeled and cut into thick 2-inch slices

1/4 cup apricot preserves

1/4 cup crushed pineapple, drained

1/4 cup concentrated orange juice, from a frozen concentrate

1 tablespoon soy sauce

1/4 teaspoon ground ginger

1/4 teaspoon pepper

Slice sweet potatoes and place them in the bottom of the slow cooker. Set pork roast on top of potato slices. In separate bowl, combine remaining ingredients and stir to blend well. Pour mixture over contents in slow cooker. Cover with lid and cook on high setting for 6 hours, or for 12 hours on low setting.

Excerpted from Crazy About Crockery! 101 Easy and Inexpensive Recipes for Less than .75 cents a serving ISBN 1891400126 by Penny E. Stone

A Tip from the Kitchen...

"When image is all..." Quick garnishes on a plate or platter make a colorful statement (and another course!) Choose spiced peaches, ruby red crab apples, sliced fresh pineapple, gingered pears, sliced kiwi, clusters of mini purple grapes, pickled mushrooms, a dollop of rustically cut salsa-cruda relish, chutney, pickled kumquats, a sliced tomato from your garden, or even nasturtium blossoms...the list is endless. Browse the fancy food section of your market and get creative, or take a stroll through your garden to pick something sun-ripened and home-grown.

Lamb Beans and Rice

6 servings

2 pounds lamb meat, cubed and fat removed
2 medium onions, finely chopped
1 stick butter
2 pounds string beans or fresh green beans, trimmed
2 teaspoons salt
1/2 teaspoon black pepper
1 quart tomato juice
1 cup water
4 cups cooked rice

In a large skillet melt the butter. Add the cubed lamb and chopped onions, cooking until meat is browned and onions are transparent (about 10 minutes). Transfer to slow cooker. Pour on the tomato juice and water, salt and pepper. Cook on high setting for 4 hours, or until meat is becoming tender. Lastly add the green beans and cook for 1 hour more, or until lamb is fork tender and beans are crisp-tender. Serve over cooked rice.

Excerpted and adapted from 365 Quick, Easy and Inexpensive Dinner Menus ISBN 1891400339 by Penny E. Stone

A Tip from the Kitchen...

When cooking rice in a slow cooker use long grain rice rather than the quick cooking varieties for best results. Like any rule, there are exceptions and a few of the recipes in this book call for instant or quick cooking rice...and some even for cooked rice. However, the general rule is to use long grain rice when possible.

Chapter Five:
Putting on the Ritz...
Parties, Holidays and Festive Foods

"Putting on the Ritz..." Elaborate entertaining doesn't have to be intimidating when you have your "instant butler" (your slow cooker) at hand. Making advanced preparation and stressful timing a cinch, you will have plenty of time to relax and enjoy your party without being a slave to the kitchen. Slow cookers 'hold' food nicely on the buffet table and make wonderful 'assistants', maximizing your cooking ability when your oven is filled to capacity--a nice quality during Holiday Seasons when you need extra room for that special side dish or second-turkey stuffing that Grandma used to make.

Parties, Holidays and Festive Foods Recipe Index

Crab Fondue Appetizer

1 stick of butter, melted
1 medium package Velveeta® cheese
1 cup shredded Cheddar cheese
1 can crab meat, drained
Dash of sherry (to taste)

Combine all ingredients in slow cooker and melt into a smooth fondue-style sauce, using high setting. Once blended, reduce setting to low to keep warm. Serve warm with Ritz® crackers for dipping.

-from the kitchen of Captain Jack Feiereisen, Dream Walker Charters

The Rush Hour Cook's Easy Chili Cheese Dip

1 can Hormel® chili without beans
1 (16 ounce) package Velveeta® cheese
Corn chips or tortilla chips, for dipping
Red pepper sauce (optional)

Put chili and cheese in slow cooker. Mix and melt on high heat setting, stirring occasionally. Turn slow cooker to low to keep dip warm while serving.
Cook's Note: Spice lovers can add red pepper sauce to taste.

Excerpted from The Rush Hour Cook presents Effortless Entertaining ISBN 189140086X by Brook Noel

(Not in a pot, but too good to pass up) Spastic Salsa

1 jar salsa (you choose the heat)
1 can Mexican corn
1 tablespoon sugar
1 chopped Jalapeno pepper
Salt and pepper to taste

Mix all ingredients together and let sit 30 minutes before serving. Use as an appetizer with tortilla chips or as a freshly-contrasting condiment or side-garnish to your slowly cooked meats.

Excerpted from The Rush Hour Cook presents Family Favorites ISBN 1891400835 by Brook Noel

Captain Jack's Peel'em and Eat'em Shrimp

3-4 pounds shrimp, in their shells
1 bottle of beer
1 tablespoon salt
2-3 tablespoons pickling spices, or shrimp-boil spices
Water to cover
Dipping sauces of choice, at serving time

Rinse the shrimp and place in slow cooker. Add remaining ingredients, mixing well. Cover with lid and cook on high setting for 1-2 hours, or until shrimp turn pink and are cooked through. Turn slow cooker to low setting and keep shrimp warm. Serve warm with a favorite condiment. Or chill the shrimp and serve cold with cocktail sauce and/or homemade mayonnaise.

—*from the kitchen of Captain Jack Feiereisen, Dream Walker Charters*

A Tip from the Kitchen...

Since we are peeling and eating in quite rustic fashion, let's get out the 'finger bowls' —remember those? A nice touch is to serve warmed water with floating lemon slices, in little bowls for each of your guests. If you don't want to go the finger bowl route use plenty of good quality napkins and extra lemon wedges, or last but not least the proverbial Handi-Wipes®.

Paella-Style Shrimp, Chicken and Sausage Dish

6 servings

1 pound boneless, skinless chicken meat, cut into strips
1/2 pound spicy Italian or Spanish sausage, cut into pieces
1/2 pound medium shrimp, shelled and de-veined
1 large onion, cut into thick slices
1 can chicken broth
1 (16 ounce) can stewed tomatoes, un-drained
1-2 garlic cloves, mashed and minced
Salt and pepper to taste
Saffron threads, for color
1 teaspoon dried oregano, crushed between your fingers
1 bay leaf
2 cups long grain rice
1 (10 ounce) package frozen tiny peas, thawed
Capers (found in condiment or fancy food section of your
   market)

Brown the sausage and chicken pieces with the onion slices
in a little olive oil in a non stick skillet and transfer to slow
cooker. Pour in the broth and tomatoes and add the spices.
Stir in the rice and saffron threads. Cover with lid and cook
on high setting for 2-4 hours, or until meats are done and
rice is plumped. Add the shrimp and the peas; cover with
lid and continue to cook until shrimp are opaque and done,
approximately another hour. Sprinkle with capers, right out
of the jar, just before serving.

—from the kitchen of Wendy Louise

A Tip from the Kitchen...

of Hannalorre ... When decorating your plate use fancy green onion frills. Choose clean crisp green onions from your market. Peel off any unsightly or tough outer skins and greens and trim both ends. With a paring knife carefully slit along each end making slivered frills about 2-3 inches long, paring horizontally from middle to end. Rotate the onion until you've made 4 to 6 horizontal cuts through each end. Immediately plunge the onion spear into ice water and the cut ends will automatically curl and frill. Store these little "fire crackers" in ice water until ready to use for garnish.

Trudy's Scalloped Oyster Pudding

6-8 servings

1 ½ pints-1 quart fresh oysters, with their juice (can
substitute canned)
1/2 large box Saltine® crackers, coarsely crumbled
1 cup milk
3 large eggs
1 stick butter, melted

Crumble crackers into a bowl. Beat the eggs and milk
together and pour over the Saltines®. Stir in the melted
butter. Fold in the oysters and their juice. Place the mixture
in a buttered slow cooker. Dot the top of the pudding with a
little butter. Cover with lid (but vent very slightly) and cook
the pudding on high setting for approximately 2-4 hours
until set, or when knife put in center comes out clean. Serve
warm.

Cook's Note: Serve as a side dish with your holiday meal
or as an elegant appetizer for a fancy dinner.

*-original recipe by Trudy Pengburn, adapted for crockery-style cooking by
Wendy Louise*

A Tip from the Kitchen...
of Brook Noel (excerpted from *The Rush Hour Cook: Weekly Wonders* ISBN 1891400142) She says, " Create a memory...with a great gift idea." Brook suggests, "that if your family has many 'heirloom' recipes collect them and create several menus as gifts. Add family pictures, journaling and anecdotes. Print on attractive paper or take to a copy store for duplication and binding."

Classic Swiss Fondue

2 quarts

1 garlic clove
2-3 cups dry Rhine, Chablis or Riesling wine
1 tablespoon lemon juice
1 pound Swiss cheese, grated
1/2 pound Cheddar cheese, grated
3 tablespoons flour
3 tablespoons Kirsch
Freshly ground nutmeg, to taste
McCormick Season-All®, to taste
1 Italian or French bread loaf, cut into 1-inch cubes

Rub an enameled or stainless steel pan with the garlic clove. Heat wine to a slow simmer and add lemon juice. Combine cheeses and flour, and gradually stir in. Stir constantly until cheese has melted. Pour into lightly greased slow cooker. Add Kirsch and stir well. Sprinkle with nutmeg and Season-All®. Cover with lid and cook on high setting for 1/2 hour, then reduce to low setting for 2-5 hours. Keep on low setting while serving. Skewer bite-sized bread cubes onto long forks and dip into warm cheese mixture. Enjoy.

Recipe contributed by Michael Gulan, Champion Press Ltd. Publishing Assistant

Brie Cheese Appetizer served with Festive Cranberry Chutney

8 servings

1 round of very good Brie cheese
Festive Cranberry Chutney (see page 205)
Very Good crackers (English soda are nice)

Variation # 1

When serving as a first course, place a wedge of room temperature Brie cheese on each plate. Serve a very generous portion of your (Festive) Cranberry Chutney (page 205), warm or cold on the side, along with very good crackers. Let each person assemble to their desire.

Variation # 2

Place the whole Brie in the oven on a greased oven proof plate. Bake at 350 degrees F. until warmed, softened and almost to the verge of melting. Top with the chutney and heat a minute (or two) more. Serve warm with good crackers.

—from the kitchen of Wendy Louise

Everyone's Favorite Party Meatballs

5 dozen

1 pound ground beef
1/2 cup dry, commercial breadcrumbs
1/3 cup finely chopped onion
1 tablespoon crushed parsley
1 teaspoon salt
1 teaspoon Worcestershire sauce
1/2 teaspoon pepper
1 egg
1 (12 ounce) bottle chili sauce
1 (10 ounce) jar grape jelly

Mix ground beef, breadcrumbs, onion, parsley, seasonings and egg together. Shape into 1-inch balls. Brown the meatballs in a skillet over medium heat for about 10 minutes, turning frequently. Drain off fat. In same pan pour chili sauce and jelly over the meatballs, stirring until jelly is melted and meatballs are coated. Transfer all to slow cooker. Cover with lid and simmer on low setting until your guests arrive. Serve warm.

Cook's Note: This recipe is best if the meatballs have at least 1 hour to simmer and to blend flavors before serving

Excerpted from The Rush Hour Cook presents Effortless Entertaining ISBN 189140086X by Brook Noel

"Christmas in July"... The Ultimate Turkey Dinner

10-12 servings

Cook's Note: This recipe calls for a turkey slowly cooked and smoked on a covered barbecue grill in the middle of July. The reason we included it was to showcase Lucile's Homemade crockery-style Stuffing (recipe to follow) and to show the similarities between the slow cooker and the covered-barbecue grill (another 'slow cooker' of sorts).

A large turkey, thawed, cleaned, and giblets removed
Salt and pepper
A covered, kettle-style barbecue grill
Hickory bark (chipped and soaked in water)
Plenty of slow cooking coals
Drip-pan
1 recipe Lucille's Crockery-style Stuffing, page 171
   (You might have to substitute canned chestnuts in the summer time or omit them altogether.)

Thaw your turkey, clean and pat dry. Season outside (and cavity) with salt and pepper. Do NOT stuff the turkey when grilling it. Make your stuffing in a slow cooker and serve along side. Prepare and arrange your coals in a ring around the barbecue grill. Place a drip pan in the center. Center your turkey over the drip pan (to catch all drippings, and to keep the fire from flaring up). Sprinkle some of the soaked hickory chips onto the coals. Put the cover on the grill, and adjust the cooking vents for a strong, but slow cooking fire.

(Fire should be maintained at approximately 250-275 degrees F.). Add more Hickory chips periodically. Refurbish coals as necessary. Resist opening the cover, as much as possible. Cooking time will range from 4-6+hours depending on size of bird, consistency of fire and weather variables. (Usually your grill comes with cooking guidelines and instructions to aid you.) Cook until all juices run clear, and meat is literally falling off the bone. A meat thermometer inserted into the thickest part of the bird should read at least 175 degrees F. (but 180 degrees F. is considered a safer temperature). The meat should be succulent and very, very tender. Remove turkey from grill and let 'set' for 30 minutes before carving. Serve with Lucille's Crockery-style Stuffing (see following page).

Lucile's Crockery Stuffing
12+ servings

12-14 cups toasted bread cubes (or day old bread, cubed)

1 pound bulk sausage, cooked, drained, and crumbled

1 pound fresh chestnuts (in season), par-boiled, skins removed, crushed and crumbled (These are optional—a lot of work, but worth the sweet, nutty flavor they bring to the stuffing!)

1/2 to 1 cup melted butter (to flavor the bread)

1 medium onion, diced fine

2 ribs celery, diced fine

1 tablespoon parsley flakes

1-2 teaspoons poultry seasoning, or to taste

Salt and pepper to taste

1 (14 1/2 ounce) can chicken broth (to moisten the dressing)

2 eggs, beaten (optional) (Some people like the addition of beaten egg, folded into their stuffing, to help 'bind it' together. I prefer not to utilize this option.)

Prepare your slow cooker with a little cooking spray. Combine bread cubes and crumbled, cooked sausage and place in your slow cooker. Melt the butter in a skillet and sauté diced onion and celery until tender. Stir in the seasonings and prepared chestnuts. Stir in the chicken broth, combining well. Pour over the bread/sausage mixture in the slow cooker and toss lightly to coat all. Cover with lid and 'bake' on high setting for 1 hour. Reduce setting to low and cook an additional 3-4 hours. Serve as a tasty side dish with your Christmas in July Turkey.

Authors Note: Turkey recipe provided by Caleb Feiereisen, the stuffing by his Grandmother Lucile, as prepared and enjoyed in Manitowish Waters, Wisconsin.

A Tip from the Kitchen...

of George Feiereisen—To peel fresh chestnuts, cut a crisscross-slash through the skin on the curved side of each nut and then parboil covered with water for 5-8 minutes, until skins begin to pull away. Drain and cool slightly to handle easily. With a sharp knife peel off the outer skins. Do not let nuts cool too much, as they are easier to peel when warm. Chop the nut meats coarsely and give to Lucile to add to the stuffing.

Scalloped Potatoes and Ham for a Crowd

20 servings

1 pound ham, cut into small cubes
5 pounds potatoes, washed and sliced with skins on
1 large onion, chopped
1 pound yellow cheese (any variety), grated
1/2 cup margarine
1/2 cup flour
4 cups milk
Salt and pepper to taste

Sauté ham with onions, until onions are transparent. Place in large slow cooker. Put sliced potatoes in slow cooker and mix together with ham and onions. In separate pan melt margarine and stir in butter to make a roux. Heat to boiling point and add milk, mixing constantly with wire whisk until thickened. Fold in grated cheese and melt to smooth sauce. Add salt and pepper to taste. Pour over potato-ham mixture and mix well. Cover with lid and cook on low 7- 8 hours, until bubbly and potatoes are tender.

Excerpted and adapted from Frozen Assets, cook for a day and eat for a month ISBN 1891400614 with Deborah Taylor-Hough

Brown-Sugar Honey Coated Ham

6-8 servings

1 good sized, precooked boneless ham
1 cup brown sugar
3/4 cup honey
1/2 cup water
1 can (regular, not diet) cola soda

Place ham in slow cooker and pour cola over ham. Turn slow cooker onto low setting and start warming the ham and cola. Meanwhile, in sauce pan, combine brown sugar, honey and water, bringing to a boil. Pour over the ham. Cover with lid and continue cooking on low setting for 6-10 hours, until ham is tender. (Or cook on high setting for approximately 3-4 hours, until ham is tender and heated through.)

Cook's Note: Serve as a complete dinner with potatoes and a side vegetable. Or slice thin and serve on Kaiser rolls to make delicious ham sandwiches (warm or cold).

Excerpted and adapted from 365 Quick, Easy and Inexpensive Dinner Menus ISBN 1891400339 by Penny E. Stone

Holiday Brisket of Beef with Cranberry-Horseradish Sauce

Makes 8-10 servings

1 (3-4 pound) center cut beef brisket, trimmed of fat
Bottled smoke
Onion salt
Garlic salt
Celery salt
Water
4-6 peppercorns
1 ½ cups barbecue sauce
Cranberry-Horseradish Sauce (next page)

Add liberal amounts of smoke and salts to both sides of the brisket, rubbing well. Place brisket in slow cooker and add a little water. Cover with lid and cook on low 8-10 hours, or until beef is fork tender. Last hour of cooking, add the barbecue sauce. Serve hot and thinly sliced (across the grain) with parsley buttered new potatoes and Cranberry-Horseradish Sauce (see recipe on next page).

A Tip from the Kitchen...

"Make wonderful scents"--by turning your slow cooker into a simmering potpourri pot. Stud some oranges with whole cloves, add a couple of cinnamon sticks, star anise, some water and simmer away. Let the scents of the season fill your house with aromatic comfort. Just be careful not to scorch the pot, since you are doing this with the cover off.

Cranberry-Horseradish Sauce

6 servings

1 pound whole cranberry sauce
2 tablespoons butter
2 tablespoons brown sugar
2 tablespoons horseradish
1 teaspoon Dijon style mustard

Heat all ingredients together, until butter and brown sugar are melted, and ingredients are incorporated. Serve warm or cold, as an accompaniment to meats; especially good with Turkey or Pork.

—from the kitchen of Joan Sennett, adapted for crockery-style cooking by Wendy Louise

A Tip from the Kitchen...

Dying Easter Eggs?—How about hard boiling them in your slow cooker first. Add a little vinegar to the water and you are 'cleaning' your pot to boot! Since these eggs will be used for **decoration only** and out of the refrigerator for a long time, undoubtedly waiting for the Easter Bunny to hide them, it is advisable not to eat them! Eggs left un-refrigerated for 3 or more hours are susceptible to bacteria. So, the eggs you plan to eat boil on the stove and store in the fridge.

March Madness Corned Beef Boiled Dinner

8 servings

1 (3 pound plus) corned beef
1-2 cups water or apple juice
1 teaspoon peppercorns
6 whole cloves
1 bay leaf
8 potatoes, peeled and quartered
8 carrots, lengthwise cut in half and chunked
1 head cabbage, cut in 8 wedges, core removed

In large slow cooker, place the potatoes and carrots. Nestle the corned beef into the pot, onto the vegetables, and pour in water or apple juice. Add peppercorns, cloves and bay leaf. Cover with lid and cook on low setting for 8-10 hours, or until meat and vegetables are nearing fork tender. Add the cabbage wedges. Cover with lid and turn setting to high. Continue cooking until cabbage is crisp-tender (about another hour).

Cook's Note: If the corned beef comes with a seasoning packet, omit peppercorns, cloves and bay leaf and use the packet instead.

Excerpted and adapted from 365 Quick, Easy and Inexpensive Dinner Menus ISBN 1891400339 by Penny E. Stone

Corned Beef Casserole

4-5 servings

1 (12 ounce) can corned beef, chopped
1/4 pound American cheese, cubed
2 cans cream of mushroom soup
1 soup can water
1 cup milk
1 medium onion, chopped
4 cups cubed raw potatoes
1-2 cups sliced carrots
1 cup sliced mushrooms (optional)
1 cup buttered crumbs or croutons

Combine all ingredients in slow cooker and stir to blend well. Cover with lid and cook on high setting for 6-8 hours.

Excerpted from Crazy About Crockery! 101 Easy and Inexpensive Recipes for less than .75 cents a serving ISBN 1891400126 by Penny E. Stone

A Tip from the Kitchen...

"Create-A-Memory-Night"—Get out old photographs and set one at each person's place setting. Have everybody share memories and tell stories about that time in their life. Add a lot of giggling, good food and fun. Or use baby photos as "place cards" and have everybody guess "who sits where".

Hoppin' John

8 servings

Cook's Note: "This traditional Southern dish is served on New Year's Day for good luck. The black eyed peas mean good luck and the greens mean money."

1 pound black-eyed peas, soaked overnight, rinsed and drained
1 tablespoon olive oil
2 onions, chopped
1 rib of celery, chopped fine
1 bell pepper, seeded and chopped
2 cloves garlic, pressed
4 cups water
3 cups chicken broth
1 teaspoon crushed pepper
1 ½ teaspoons thyme
1 teaspoon basil
1/2 teaspoon each: marjoram and oregano
1 pound turkey sausage, cooked and crumbled
Salt and pepper to taste
Cooked brown rice for serving

In a skillet, heat the oil and add onions, celery and bell pepper. Cook till wilted, stirring often to prevent sticking. Add the garlic, lower heat and cook for another minute. In a slow cooker, place the black-eyed peas, the cooked veggies from the skillet, the water, the chicken broth, crushed pepper, and the rest of the seasonings. Cover with lid and cook on low setting for about 8 hours. Add the cooked and crumbled sausage, and salt and pepper to taste. Serve with bowls of brown rice. **Cook's Note:** "Happy New Year, even if you are making this in the middle of October!"

Excerpted from The Frantic Family Cookbook (mostly) healthy meals in minutes ISBN 1891400118 By Leanne Ely, C.N.C.

A Tip from the Kitchen...

"Make it a party"—While your dinner slow-cooks make the decorations. Have your kids make holiday placemats and laminate them at the copy store. Put their creativity to work and make a theme centerpiece to match...and even place cards too. My granddaughter loves to decorate our table!...even if it's just picking a wild flower bouquet or leaving little notes for everybody.

Rock Cornish Game Hens

4 servings

4 Rock Cornish game hens, thawed
2 teaspoons salt
3/4 teaspoon black pepper
1 stick butter, melted
1 teaspoon paprika
1 large jar currant jelly

Place game hens in slow cooker. Drizzle melted butter over hens. Sprinkle with salt, pepper and paprika. Cover with lid and cook on high setting for 4 hours. Spoon currant jelly over each hen, letting the jelly melt and glaze each bird. Return lid to slow cooker and continue cooking on the high setting for 2-3 hours more, or until hens are extremely tender.

Excerpted from Crazy About Crockery! 101 Easy and Inexpensive Recipes for Less than .75 cents a serving ISBN 1891400126 by Penny E. Stone

A Tip from the Kitchen...

"Make any day a holiday"...think of those Cornish game hens as mini turkeys. Family too small to cook a large turkey? Serve each person their own 'mini turkey' with all the fixings. Alone for the Holiday?—cook one up for yourself, or invite a neighbor and make two. Bake two sweet potatoes in the microwave, open a can of cranberry sauce, add a spiced peach half and voila—you never even touched your oven!

A Tip from the Kitchen...

Enjoy your Holidays—That goes for the cook as well! Don't be a prisoner in your kitchen...use your slow cooker! Serve your meal directly from the pot, making it the centerpiece of your table. While prepping your meal, draw a sink full of soapy water and "clean up prep dishes as you go"... Avoid after-dinner-penance at the dishwasher by taking advantage of the beautiful paper plates, napkins and bowls (and even disposable serving containers) available to us today, making clean up a breeze. If you do have dishes or pans that need soaking, put them in their "sudsy bath" **before** you sit down to eat. When the meal is done you can retire to the living room right along with your guests, knowing full well a disastrous kitchen and piles of dishes are not lurking in the background.

Chapter Six:
Side Dishes to
'Round-Out' Your Meal

Twenty-five reasons not to forget our fruits and vegetables.

Side Dishes Recipe Index

A Really Good Ratatouille
6-8 servings

1 large eggplant, peeled and cut into bite-sized pieces
1 large onion, diced
1 green pepper, cut into bite-sized pieces
1 large zucchini, unpeeled and sliced into medallions
4 tomatoes, peeled and diced (or use canned)
3 cloves garlic, minced
1/4 -1/2 cup olive oil
12 large black olives, pitted and halved
1 bay leaf
Thyme to taste
Salt and pepper to taste

In a non stick pan lightly brown the onions in olive oil, adding the green pepper and garlic. Add the eggplant and zucchini, mixing well. Continue to cook for 5 minutes. Transfer the sautéed vegetables to slow cooker and add the tomatoes, black olives and all seasonings. Gently toss to mix all. Cover with lid and simmer on low setting for at least 1 hour, or until vegetables are fork tender, but not mushy. Serve warm. Keeps up to 1 week in the refrigerator.

Cook's Note: Excellent side dish served warm with lamb or grilled meats; or served cold as a salad or first course.

—from the kitchen of Joan Sennett, adapted for crockery-style cooking by Wendy Louise

Red Cabbage and Wine

6-8 servings

1 (2 pound head) red cabbage
4 tart apples, cored and quartered
1 cup red wine
1/3 cup firmly packed brown sugar
1 teaspoon salt
Dash cayenne pepper
1/4 cup apple cider vinegar
1/4 cup butter, melted

Wash and remove outer leaves from cabbage. Quarter the head and discard the core. Coarsely slice or shred the cabbage. Place shredded cabbage and apples in slow cooker and pour over remaining ingredients. Cover with lid and cook on low setting for 8 hours, or on high setting for 3 hours. Stir well before serving.

Excerpted and adapted from 365 Quick, Easy and Inexpensive Dinner Menus ISBN 1891400339 by Penny E. Stone

Braised Onions

6-8 servings

6-8 medium-large sweet onions, peeled and both ends
   trimmed
2 tablespoons butter
1 cup vegetable broth, chicken broth or wine (white or red)
   (if using wine, mix with a little water)
Salt and pepper to taste

In a sauté pan cook the whole onions in the butter until
well-glazed and golden. Place the onions side by side into a
greased slow cooker. Pour on the broth or wine/water.
Cover with lid and cook on low setting for 10 hours. If
necessary remove lid toward end of cooking to reduce and
caramelize the sauce. Serve as a side dish with roasted or
grilled meats.

-from the kitchen of my namesake, Great Aunt Louise

Corn on the Cob

Select freshly picked ears of corn. Pull back husks and
remove silk. Replace husks back around corn. Trim off
excess stalks to make level bottoms. Stand ears upright in
slow cooker. Pour in a small amount of water
(approximately 1/2-1 cup) Cover with lid and steam on low
setting for 2-3 hours. Pull back the husks, slather with
butter, salt and pepper to taste and eat immediately!

Cook's Note: Serve with Brats 'N Beer (see page 110)

—from the kitchen of Caleb Feiereisen

Beans Beans Beans

6 servings

1 (31 ounce) can baked beans
1 (16 ounce) can kidney beans
1 (16 ounce) can black beans
1 (16 ounce) can butter beans
1 (16 ounce) can lima beans
1 (16 ounce) can navy beans
1 onion, finely chopped
2-3 tablespoons brown sugar
1/2 cup catsup
1/2 tablespoon minced garlic, or garlic powder
1 teaspoon pepper
4 strips thick bacon

Lay bacon strips on bottom of slow cooker. Mix rest of ingredients and add to slow cooker. Cover with lid and cook on low setting for 6-8 hours. Serve hot.

—*from the kitchen of Miz Malibu*

Auntie Mae's 'Baked' Acorn or Butternut Squash

Acorn or butternut squash, halved, then quartered
1 pat of butter for each piece
1 tablespoon brown sugar for each piece
1 dusting of nutmeg for each piece
Salt and pepper to taste

Cut squash into the uniform, serving-sized pieces and remove seeds. Do not peel. Dab each with butter, brown sugar and nutmeg. Wrap individually in foil and stack in slow cooker. Do not add any water. Cover with lid and cook on high setting for 5 hours, or on low setting for 6-8 hours. Carefully remove from slow cooker and carefully remove foil. Salt and pepper to taste. Serve warm.

—from the kitchen of Mae Perdue, who introduced me to Southern Fried Chicken (that'll have to wait for another book) and baked butternut squash... hmm... hmm... hmm... could she cook!

Green Bean Side Dish

6 servings

2 packages frozen green beans, thawed
1 small onion, finely chopped
1 can cream of mushroom soup
1/2 cup milk
2 teaspoons Worcestershire sauce
1 small can French fried onions

Combine first 5 ingredients, blending well, and place in greased slow cooker. Cover with lid and cook on low setting for 5 hours. Just before serving sprinkle with the French fried onions, straight out of the can or crisped in the oven.

—from the kitchen of Wendy Louise

The Rush Hour Cook's Ravishing Vegetable Medley

6 servings

1 cup each of zucchini, carrots, broccoli, cauliflower, onion,
   green pepper and yellow squash, cut into bite-sized
pieces
1/4 cup olive oil
2 tablespoons red wine vinegar (optional)
2 tablespoons minced garlic
1 teaspoon salt
1 tablespoon pepper
1 tablespoon oregano

Place the bite-sized vegetables in the slow cooker. Mix
remaining ingredients together and toss with the vegetables
to coat evenly. Cover with lid and cook on high heat setting
for approximately 2 hours, or until vegetables are fork
tender but firm, adding a little water if necessary. Stir once,
halfway through cooking. Serve warm.

*Excerpted and adapted from The Rush Hour Cook presents Effortless
Entertaining ISBN 189140086X by Brook Noel*

MaryAnn's Baked Vegetable Dish

6-8 servings

1 package frozen broccoli, thawed
1 package frozen cauliflower, thawed
1 package mixed frozen vegetables, thawed
1 small jar (approximately 6-8 ounces) Cheez Whiz®
1 can cream of mushroom soup
1 can cream of broccoli soup
1 large can Durkee® onion rings

Place all vegetables in large slow cooker. Mix Cheez Whiz® with soups and pour over vegetables. Cover with lid and bake on high setting for 3 hours. Top with the Durkee® onion rings; cover with lid and bake on high setting for 1 more hour.

Recipe contributed by MaryAnn Koopmann, Career Woman and Homemaker

Tammy's Hot Vegetable Casserole

6-8 servings

2 packages frozen broccoli, thawed
1 can cream of mushroom soup
1/4 cup chopped onion
1 1/3 cups minute-style rice
1 (8 ounce) jar Cheez Whiz®
1 can sliced water chestnuts, drained

Mix first 5 ingredients in greased slow cooker. Cover with lid and cook on high setting for 3 hours. Add water chestnuts for last 45 minutes of cooking, so they will be crisp tender.

Recipe submitted by MaryAnn Koopmann, Career Woman and Homemaker

A Tip from the Kitchen...

Making a side dish or vegetable casserole? Don't have room in the oven? Make it in your slow cooker instead and keep it warm while you are cooking everything else. The General Rule of Thumb for Conversion—slow cooking is 1 hour of conventional cooking multiplied by 2 for High setting, or multiplied by 4 for Low setting.

Old Fashioned Stewed Tomatoes with Zucchini

8-10 servings

2 medium zucchini, cleaned but peel left on, sliced into
   discs
1 small onion, chopped
2 (14.5 ounce) cans stewed whole tomatoes, with juice
1 teaspoon dried basil, crushed between your fingers

Place all in slow cooker, cover with lid and 'stew' on low or high setting until zucchini are tender, but still hold their shape. Break up tomatoes lightly with a fork at end of cooking. Serve the stewed vegetables warm, as a side dish in little bowls. Let each person salt and pepper their portion to their taste.

—*from the kitchen of my namesake, Great Aunt Louise*

'Baked' Potatoes

6 servings

6 medium baking potatoes, scrubbed clean and left whole

Wrap each potato in aluminum foil. Stack the wrapped potatoes in slow cooker. Do not add any liquid. Cover with lid and cook on high setting for 6 hours, or low setting for 10 hours.

—*from the kitchen of Wendy Louise*

Aunt Sally's Potatoes

8 servings

Aunt Sally traditionally bakes this potato dish during the holiday season, when oven capacity is filled to the maximum. We have converted this recipe for crockery-style cooking, to conveniently create more space in the oven, for all those other yummy dishes.

1 red onion, sliced
1 (32 ounce) package of frozen hash-browns, thawed
1 (8 ounce) package shredded cheddar cheese
1 (10.75 ounce) can cream of chicken soup, undiluted
2 tablespoons butter, melted
1 teaspoon garlic powder
Salt and pepper to taste
1 (8 ounce) container sour cream, not low fat
1 can of Durkees® fried onions

Mix all ingredients together, except sour cream and Durkees® onions. Place in greased slow cooker and cover with lid. Cook 5 to 7 hours on low setting, until potatoes are fork tender and cheese is melted. During last 15-30 minutes of cooking time, stir in sour cream, and keep heating till warmed through. Bake the Durkees® fried onions in the oven for a few minutes to warm and crisp. Sprinkle on top of the potatoes just before serving to make a crispy garnish.

—from the kitchen of Aunt Sally Wise, adapted for crockery-style cooking by Wendy Louise

Parsley Boiled New Potatoes

6-8 servings

1-2 pounds medium sized red potatoes
1/4 -1/2 cup water
Melted butter to taste
Fresh parsley, finely chopped
Salt and pepper to taste

Pare a strip of peel from around the middle of each tender skinned potato. Place the potatoes and water in the slow cooker. Cover with lid and cook on high 1 ½ -3 hours, or until fork tender (but not mushy). Time will depend on size of potatoes. (You can add a little lemon juice to the water to preserve color. Potatoes have a tendency to darken over prolonged cooking or holding time.) At serving time drain and toss the potatoes with melted butter and fresh parsley. Salt and pepper to taste. Serve warm as a side dish.

—from the kitchen of Hannalorre

A Tip from the Kitchen...

When converting sliced potatoes to a slow cooker recipe, slice them very thin as they take longer to cook than in conventional cooking. Use less liquid than the original recipe calls for. Adjust seasonings at end of cooking.

The Rush Hour Cook's Dijon Potatoes

8 servings

8 baking potatoes, peeled and sliced thin
5 tablespoons flour
2 ½ cups milk
1/2 to 3/4 cup Dijon-style mustard, or to taste
5 tablespoons butter
1 cup shredded Swiss cheese
Salt and white pepper to taste

In a sauce pan make a roux of the butter and flour, cooking for a few minutes. Slowly add the milk, stirring all the while. Cook gently until the sauce thickens. Add in the mustard. Set aside. Place the sliced potatoes into a greased slow cooker. Pour the sauce over the potatoes and stir to mix. Cover with lid and cook on high setting for 1 hour, then reduce to low setting for 4-6 hours more, or until potatoes are tender. During last hour of cooking adjust seasoning with salt and white pepper if necessary. Then sprinkle the shredded Swiss cheese on the top, re-cover and continue to cook for that last hour.

Excerpted and adapted from The Rush Hour Cook: Weekly Wonders ISBN 1891400142 by Brook Noel

A Sweet Potato Casserole
6-8 servings

2 (16 ounce) cans sweet potatoes or yams, drained and
    mashed
1/2 cup fresh orange juice or apple juice
1/2 stick butter, melted
1 teaspoon grated orange peel
1/4 teaspoon allspice or pumpkin pie spice
Salt and white pepper to taste
2 large eggs, well beaten

Beat drained and mashed yams with all ingredients, except
beaten eggs, until smooth and blended. Then beat-in the
beaten eggs. When all is blended, pour into a greased or
non-stick sprayed slow cooker. Cover with lid and cook on
high setting for 1 hour, then reduce setting to low and cook
for 3-4 hours more. Serve as a side dish for holiday meals.

—from the kitchen of Wendy Louise

A Tip from the Kitchen...
of June Kirzan—When garnishing with toasted almonds
try a flavored variety for extra flair and flavor (such as
honey toasted almonds). No reason why they have to be
plain!

Fancy Wild Rice

8-10 servings

2 cups raw wild rice (The grains should be long and shiny
  dark brown; avoid dried-out-looking, small or broken
  kernels.)
1/2 cup finely minced onion
6 cups chicken broth or water
1 garlic clove, smashed and minced
1 (12 ounce) can mushrooms, pieces or sliced, drained
1/2 cup white raisins
1/2 cup toasted or slivered almonds
Salt and pepper to taste

Rinse and drain the wild rice. Put in slow cooker along with
onion, garlic and broth. Cover with lid and cook on low
setting 4-6 hours, or until rice is plumped and tender. Last
hour of cooking fold in the mushrooms and raisins. Just
before serving fold in almonds and adjust salt and pepper
to taste. —*from the kitchen of Wendy Louise*

A Tip from the Kitchen. . .
Don't have a trivet with a candle-warmer, or a plate
warmer? Cook your casserole the conventional way and
then transfer (and arrange) into a greased slow cooker to
keep warm for serving. Garnish the top of your newly
arranged casserole with Parmesan cheese, fresh snipped
parsley or toasted almonds, etc. You may 'hold' foods on
the low setting without fear of scorching or drying out,
during extended serving on a buffet table. **Do not**,
however, reheat any leftovers in the slow cooker—best to
discard at the end of the evening.

Fancy Pickled Button Mushrooms

8-10 servings

1-2 pounds firm, white button mushrooms, stems trimmed
   flush with caps
1 red onion, minced or finely diced
1-2 cloves garlic, smashed and minced
1/2 cup cider or tarragon vinegar
1/2 cup olive oil
1-2 cups white wine
1 teaspoon mixed pickling spices
1 or 2 bay leaves
Several whole black peppercorns
1/2 teaspoon salt

Place all in slow cooker and
cover with lid. Simmer on high
setting for 1-3 hours, or until
mushrooms are 'pickled' but
tender-firm. Store refrigerated
in sterilized jars. Serve cold as
an appetizer or with cocktails.

—*from the kitchen of Wendy Louise*

Cook's Note: To prepare garlic cloves see *Kitchen Tip* on page 128.

Hot Fruit Compote

6 - 8 servings

1 medium can pineapple slices
1 medium can peaches
1 jar apple rings
1 medium can pears
1 medium can apricots
2 tablespoons flour
1/2 cup brown sugar
1 stick butter
1 cup sherry (or juice)

Drain all of the fruits, saving the juice for another recipe (perhaps to use in a JELL-O ®-mold, instead of water; or in a cake, instead of milk). Arrange the fruits (in any order) in your slow cooker and turn to the low heat setting. In a small sauce pan, placed in a water-bath (or a double boiler) make a thick sauce by melting the butter, sugar and flour together, stirring constantly until blended and smooth. Stir in the cup of sherry (or you could substitute 1+ cup of the drained fruit juice) making a smooth sauce. Pour the sauce over the fruits in the slow cooker. Cover with lid and simmer the compote on low or high setting for 1-3 hours to meld flavors. Turn to low setting to hold for serving. Serve the compote warm and bubbling along side your favorite entrée.

Cook's Note: This side dish makes an elegant accompaniment for chicken, turkey and wild game, and is very easy to make—as there is no critical timing involved. The dish may also be assembled the night before and warmed on day of serving...a nice feature during the busy holiday season.

—from the kitchen of Wendy Louise

Lucile's Homemade Apple Sauce

Cook's Note: In the fall and winter, this side dish makes a great accompanying garnish for pork roasts and pork chops. Like most old-fashioned recipes, there are no particular measurements used.

Freshly picked apples, peeled and coarsely chopped
Sugar, to taste
Dash of cinnamon, to taste
Water or apple juice, for simmering

Place all in slow cooker. Cover with lid and cook on high setting for approximately 3 hours, or until apples are blended and softened. (You may mash them smooth or leave chunkier as in home-style sauce.) Turn slow cooker to low setting and keep the sauce warm until serving time.

Cook's Note: Serve warm with roast pork and potato pancakes.

—from the kitchen of Lucile Feiereisen

Crock-style Applesauce
6 servings

3 pounds Gala or Jonathan apples, peeled and quartered
1 cinnamon stick or 1 ½ teaspoons cinnamon
Pats of butter (optional)
Sucanat® (optional)

Place peeled and quartered apples, along with the
cinnamon, in slow cooker. Cover with lid and cook on high
setting for about 3 hours, or until apples are fork tender.
Serve warm in bowls. For an
extra special touch, put a pat of
butter on each serving and
sprinkle with a little Sucanat.

--Excerpted from Healthy Foods, an
irreverent guide to understanding
nutrition and feeding your family well
ISBN1891400207 by Leanne Ely, C.N.C.

Festive Cranberry Chutney

2 quarts

2 pounds fresh whole cranberries
10 whole cloves
2 (3 inch) cinnamon sticks
1/4 teaspoon salt
1/4 cup cider vinegar
1 ½ cups sugar
1/4 cup water
1 ½ cups dark raisin
1 (10 ounce) package chopped dates
1-2 tablespoons orange flavored liquor (optional)

Combine first 7 ingredients in slow cooker. Cover and cook on low setting for 4 hours, or until cranberries have popped and mixture thickens. Remove lid and stir in the dates and raisins. Turn heat to high setting and cook, uncovered, for 30-60 minutes, stirring occasionally. Lastly, stir in the orange liquor (optional). The chutney should be quite thick, and the dates chewy. Ladle into hot sterilized mason jars and store in a cool, dark pantry.

Cook's Note: Serve at room temperature, as a condiment for grilled meats or as an accompaniment for soft cheeses such as Brie Cheese Appetizer (see page 167).

—from the kitchen of Wendy Louise

A Tip from the Kitchen...

Chutneys are great for holiday gift giving and hostess gifts, instead of the usual bottle of wine. Decorate the jar and give the hostess serving suggestions included with the gift.

Cranberry-Pear Relish
8 servings

1 pound fresh cranberries
1 cup water
2 cups sugar
1 tart apple, peeled and chopped
1 pear, chopped
1 teaspoon cinnamon
1 teaspoon ginger
1 teaspoon grated orange zest
1 teaspoon grated lemon zest
1/2 cup chopped walnuts (optional)

Place cranberries, water and sugar in slow cooker. Cover with lid and cook on high heat setting until the cranberries are plumped and popped. Add the chopped apple, chopped pear, spices and zests. Cover again and cook an additional 30-45 minutes to blend flavors. Do not let apple and pear become mushy—as this is more a relish than a sauce. Lastly, fold in 1/2 cup chopped walnuts (optional). Cool. (You can refrigerate for up to 1 week.) Serve as a cold relish, or with Brie Cheese Appetizer, on page 167.

—from the kitchen of Joan Sennett

A Tip from the Kitchen...

Any of these chutneys, relishes and compotes may be stored in sterilized jars, in your pantry or refrigerator and are great for gift giving. Immediately ladle your recipe (while piping hot) into sterilized jars and promptly screw on self-sealing caps. As the jars cool the caps will indent, forming a proper seal. Before filling, your jars may be sterilized in the dishwasher! —or (the old fashioned way) placed upside-down in a tray if 1-inch boiling water on the stove top. Literally boil and steam the jars (throw the caps in there too, and your ladle) for about 10 minutes just prior to filling. Using tongs, carefully remove jars from 'water bath' and invert on paper towels. The steam and water droplets will automatically evaporate from the jars, leaving clean, dry interiors. Proceed with filling, wiping any drips and spills from the rims, so you have a 'clean seal'. I know this sounds like quite the process, but it's really fun—and once you've done it, you'll be a pro. Add decorations and serving suggestions on little tags with your gifts.

"Platinum Blonde" Curried Fruit

8-10 servings

1/3 cup melted butter
3/4 cup brown sugar
2-3 teaspoons curry
  powder
1 jar maraschino cherries

1 large can of each fruit:
  Peaches
  Pears
  Apricots
  Pineapple

Drain the fruits and place in slow cooker. Combine the melted butter, brown sugar and curry powder, and add to the slow cooker. Toss all to coat. Cover with lid and simmer on low setting for 2 hours, or until flavors have blended and compote is heated through.

Excerpted from Cooking for Blondes: gourmet recipes for the culinarily challenged ISBN 1891400940 by Rhonda Levitch

Alsace Lorraine Apple Butter

6-10 pints

4 quarts finely chopped, tart cooking apples
2 cups apple cider
3 cups sugar
3 teaspoons cinnamon
1/2 teaspoon ground cloves (optional)
Pinch of salt

Put ingredients in slow cooker in order listed. Stir to blend. Cover with lid and cook on high setting for 3 hours, stirring occasionally. Reduce heat to low setting and continue to cook, covered but vented with a toothpick, for 10-12 hours more, stirring occasionally. The butter is done when it reduces to a thickened 'jam' with dark brown color. Pour into hot sterilized jars (see page 206) and seal immediately. Store in a cool, dark pantry. Serve on crumpets, or slather on scones.

—from the kitchen of my namesake, Great Aunt Louise

Chapter Seven
The Finishing Touches...
Desserts and Beverages

The finishing touches... Dessert time, that sweet time at the end of your meal time—the perfect time to receive your standing ovation with a memorable dessert, served warm and bubbling from your slow cooker— your grand finale to your perfectly orchestrated meal.

Desserts and Beverages Recipe Index

Cheryl's Sherried Pears Served with Crème Fraiche

Cook's serving suggestion: 1 pear (i.e. 2 halves per person)

Winter pears, peeled, halved and cored (I like to use Bosch pears)
Butter
Strawberry jam
Brown sugar
Macaroons, crumbled
Sherry (or water)

Arrange halved, peeled, cored winter pears (cored-side up) in a buttered slow cooker. As you make each layer dot each pear half (in their centers) with butter, a dab of strawberry jam, a pinch of brown sugar and a dab of crumbled macaroon (optional). Sprinkle with a little sherry (or water). Cover with lid and simmer on low setting 1-3 hours or until pears are fork tender, but still hold their shape. Add a little more sherry or water only if necessary. To serve, place 2 pear halves on a dessert plate and garnish with additional crumbled macaroons and any of the remaining cooking juices. Serve warm with a garnish of whipped cream, sour cream, an ice cream of your choice, or crème fraiche.

—from the kitchen of a college friend, submitted by Wendy Louise

Crème Fraiche

1 cup heavy (whipping) cream
2 tablespoons buttermilk or yogurt

Combine all in a glass container and let sit, on an undisturbed counter at room temperature for 5-8 hours, or overnight to thicken. Use in place of sour cream, on desserts or in sauces. Once the crème fraiche has 'proofed' you can refrigerate for up to 1 week in a covered glass container.

Cook's Side Note: Not only for desserts, crème fraiche has an additional advantage (over sour cream) in that it can be boiled, simmered and reduced with little risk of curdling in heated sauces.

Penny's Peach Cobbler

6 servings

1 stick butter or margarine, melted
1 cup sugar
1 cup flour
2 teaspoons baking powder
3/4 cup milk
2 cups sliced fresh peaches (or canned)
1 cup sugar

Pour melted butter or margarine into slow cooker and swirl around to coat bottom and sides. In bowl combine first cup of sugar, flour, baking powder and milk; beat on high with electric mixer. Pour flour mixture into slow cooker. Don't stir. Next, spoon peaches on top of flour mixture, then sprinkle with second cup of sugar. Cover with a clean terry-cloth kitchen towel and set slow cooker lid over towel. (Towel will help absorb excess moisture.) Cook on low setting for 3-4 hours. Serve warm with rich vanilla ice cream.

Excerpted from Crazy About Crockery! 101 Recipes for Entertaining at Less than .75 cents a serving ISBN 1891400525 by Penny E. Stone

Mother's Glazed Dessert Peaches

1 fresh peach (2 halves) per person
Butter
Dark brown sugar
Sherry (optional)
Half-and-half cream (for serving)

Peel, pit and halve the peaches. Place in buttered slow cooker with hollowed sides up. Fill each peach center with a dab of butter and a pinch of dark brown sugar. Can sprinkle on sherry if you want. Cover with lid and heat on high setting until peaches are warmed, glazed and tender, but still hold their shape. Serve warm in small dessert bowls. Pour on a little half-and-half cream and you'll think you're in heaven.

—from the kitchen of Betty Tillman

Blueberry Delight

6 servings

1/2 stick butter or margarine, melted
1 cup sugar
1 cup Bisquick® or self-rising flour
1 cup milk
1 can prepared blueberry pie-filling fruit

In a bowl, combine melted butter or margarine with sugar, Bisquick® and milk. Pour batter into slow cooker. Pour canned fruit in center, do not stir. Cover top of slow cooker with clean terry-cloth kitchen towel and place lid over slow cooker. Cook on high setting for 2-3 hours. Scoop out and serve warm, topped with a scoop of vanilla ice cream.

Excerpted from Crazy About Crockery! 101 Recipes for Entertaining at Less than .75 cents a serving ISBN 1891400525 by Penny E. Stone

Cherries Jubilee

4-8 servings

1 or 2 cans pitted dark sweet cherries, drained with juice
   reserved
1 or 2 tablespoons cornstarch
1/4 cup brandy

Place the drained cherries in the slow cooker. Dissolve the
cornstarch in the reserved cherry juice and pour over the
cherries. Cover with lid and heat on low setting until sauce
is thickened and cherries are heated through. When ready
to serve, ignite 1/4 cup brandy in a ladle. When the flames
die down, pour onto cherry-sauce mixture and gently
incorporate. Serve sauce warm, over rich vanilla ice cream
in your fanciest dessert bowls or stemmed glasses.

—this one's for you Caleb!--from the kitchen of Wendy Louise

Fresh Rhubarb Cobbler

6 servings

4 cups fresh rhubarb, washed and diced
1 ¼ cups sugar
3 tablespoons butter or margarine, melted
2 eggs, beaten
2 teaspoons lemon juice
2 cups Bisquick®
1 cup sugar
1/2 cup brown sugar
1/2 cup milk
1 ½ teaspoons baking powder
1/2 teaspoon ground cinnamon

Combine cut rhubarb with 1 ¼ cups sugar, 3 tablespoons melted butter or margarine, lemon juice and the 2 eggs in bottom of slow cooker. Stir to mix well. In a separate bowl, combine all remaining ingredients and mix well. Pour the Bisquick® mixture over the fruit mixture. Do not stir. Cover with a clean terry-cloth kitchen towel and set slow cooker lid over towel. Cook on low setting for 3-4 hours.

Excerpted from Crazy About Crockery! 101 Recipes for Entertaining at Less than .75 cents a serving ISBN 1891400525 by Penny E. Stone

A Tip from the Kitchen...
of Penny E. Stone, *Crazy About Crockery!*
When 'baking' desserts in your slow cooker, take a tip from Penny and place a clean terry-cloth kitchen towel over the pot before you put on the lid. "The towel will help absorb excess moisture." She also says for a prettier effect, "Serve

the dessert in individual bowls topped with ice cream or whipped cream—instead of letting each person scoop directly from the pot. Although crockery-style desserts have tremendous flavor and rich taste—they do not look quite as pretty as their baked counterparts when they are presented directly from the slow cooker."

Oriental Fruit Dessert
6 servings

2 cups sugar
6 eggs, beaten
2 sticks butter or margarine, melted
2 cups raisins
1 cup flaked coconut
2 cups chopped nuts
1 tablespoon lemon juice

Combine all ingredients and pour into slow cooker. Cover with lid and cook on low for 3 hours.

Excerpted from Crazy About Crockery! 101 Recipes for Entertaining at Less than .75 cents a serving ISBN 1891400525 by Penny E. Stone

Fruit Cocktail Pudding

6 servings

1 ½ cups flour
1 cup sugar
1 teaspoon baking soda
1/2 teaspoon salt
1 egg, slightly beaten
1 (2 pound) can fruit cocktail with juice
1 cup brown sugar
1/2 cup chopped nuts

Sift together flour with sugar, baking soda and salt. Add egg and beat to form smooth batter. Add fruit cocktail, with juice, and blend well. Pour into greased slow cooker. Sprinkle brown sugar and chopped nuts over batter. Cover with a clean terry-cloth kitchen towel and set slow cooker lid over towel. Cook on low setting for 3-4 hours. Serve with ice cream or whipped cream.

Excerpted from Crazy About Crockery! 101 Recipes for Entertaining at Less than .75 cents a serving ISBN 1891400525 by Penny E. Stone

Mocha Fondue

6-8 servings

20 ounces of fine quality sweet milk chocolate, broken into
  pieces
1 cup heavy cream
1-2 tablespoons (or to taste) of instant coffee or instant
  espresso powder

Place chocolate pieces in slow cooker and cook on high
setting until chocolate melts, stirring constantly. Turn slow
cooker to low setting. Incorporate the coffee powder and
heavy cream,until smooth. Continue to keep warm on low
setting while serving. Serve with bite-sized pieces of:
banana, fresh pineapple, pound cake, angel food cake,
donut holes, marshmallows, whole strawberries or chunks
of dense brownie –or whatever you can think of, to get that
chocolate on your fork! Skewer desired item and dip into
the warm fondue to coat. Eat immediately.

Cook's Note: Definitely not 'fat free' this is a sinful dessert
for the chocolate lover!

—this one's for you Brook! --from the kitchen of Wendy Louise

A Tip from the Kitchen...
When serving warm, cobbler-style and pudding-style
desserts scoop them into individual serving dishes and top
with a "fresh" and contrasting topping, such as freshly
whipped heavy cream, rich vanilla ice cream, cinnamon ice
cream or crème fraiche (see recipe on page 212). Sprinkle-
on toasted nuts, toasted macaroons, freshly grated coconut,

or a crunched-up candy bar for texture and crunch. Perhaps add a slice of the fresh version of the fruit itself (that was cooked in the dessert) or even a contrasting fruit such as a slice of kiwi, fresh berries or a sprig of mint. That little "finishing touch" can add the pizzazz that makes the ending of your meal memorable. —Or maybe it's just presenting the dessert in pretty long-stemmed glasses, instead of your every day bowls. Make dessert special; give it your signature, your personal flair.

The Rush Hour Cook's Fondue for You

1 (14 ounce) can condensed milk
1 cup semi-sweet chocolate chips
Milk, if needed

Combine chocolate and condensed milk, stirring constantly until melted and smooth. Keep warm on low setting for serving. Add milk to thin to desired consistency, if needed.

Serve as a dipping sauce for:

	Marshmallows
Strawberries	Cantaloupe
Graham crackers	Angel food cake
Bananas	Lady fingers

Excerpted from The Rush Hour Cook presents Effortless Entertaining ISBN 189140086X by Brook Noel

A Tip from the Kitchen...

Melting chocolate?—Don't have room for a double boiler on the stove?—Use your slow cooker!

Dessert Dipped Strawberries

Choice fresh strawberries, left whole and stems on (for little
  handles)
Fine quality chocolate for melting
Waxed paper

Carefully melt chocolate on low setting. Dip the whole
berries half to three-quarters the way up in the chocolate.
Lay in single layer on a cookie sheet lined with waxed paper
and store in the refrigerator. The chocolate coating will set
firm as it cools. Serve on doily-lined plates.

Cook's Side Note: You can also do this with pretzels,
coating them halfway into white or dark chocolate, using
the exposed halves as 'handles'. Store pretzels in airtight
container once cooled.

-from the kitchen of Hannalorre

Baked Apple Pudding

8 servings

6 cups tart apples, cored, peeled and sliced
1 ½ cups sugar
1/2 cup brown sugar
1 tablespoon ground cinnamon
1/2 teaspoon nutmeg
1/4 teaspoon ground ginger
1 pint half-and-half
1 stick butter or margarine
1 teaspoon baking powder
1 cup flour
1 tablespoon cornstarch
1/2 teaspoon salt
2 cups water

Peel and core apples. Slice into slow cooker. In a separate bowl, combine sugars, cinnamon, nutmeg, ginger, baking powder, flour and salt. Mix well. Melt butter and add to dry mixture. Then stir in the half-and-half. Dissolve the cornstarch in the 2 cups water and add to the flour-mixture. Stir to mix well. Add to slow cooker and stir to blend both fruit and dough mixture together. Cover with clean terry-cloth kitchen towel and set slow cooker lid over towel. Cook on low setting for 4-5 hours. Stir before serving and serve warm with rich vanilla ice cream or cinnamon ice cream.

Excerpted from Crazy About Crockery! 101 Recipes for Entertaining at Less than .75 cents a serving ISBN 1891400525 by Penny E. Stone

The Story Lady's Sweet Caramel Custard

6-8 servings

4 medium eggs
1 teaspoon vanilla
3 ½ cups whole milk
4 ½ cups granulated sugar, divided
1/2 cup boiling water
Butter

Beat the eggs with an electric beater until thick. Add the vanilla and continue beating until lemon colored. Add the milk and 2 ½ cups of the sugar, and with the beater on low continue combining well. Set aside. Butter a 2 quart mold and set aside. In a heavy, medium-sized skillet melt the remaining 2 cups sugar over very low heat. When it begins to bubble and turn brown, stir to combine all the melting sugar in the skillet. When the caramelizing sugar is medium brown, pour half the caramelizing mixture into the bottom of the buttered mold; set aside. And into the other half of the caramelized sugar, pour the 1/2 cup boiling water. Continue to stir over low heat until mixture bubbles again; allow it to cool, then chill for use as sauce. Now pour the beaten egg mixture (that you had set aside) into the buttered mold. Place a small trivet or rack in the bottom of the slow cooker, pour in 2 cups of boiling water and gently place the filled mold down into the water-bath in the slow cooker. Cover the slow cooker with the lid propped open just slightly (to vent excess steam). Cook on high setting for 4 hours, or until knife inserted in center of the custard comes out clean. When done, carefully remove the molded custard from the slow cooker and set aside to cool. Then chill, covered in refrigerator. At serving time invert and un-mold. Serve with the reserved caramel sauce.

—from the kitchen of Bonnie Gulan, Writer,Historian, Story Lady and perhaps of Royal Russian Descent

Brazilian Hot Chocolate
8 servings

2/3 cup cocoa
1 cup sugar
2 tablespoons instant coffee granules
3 cinnamon sticks
1/2 teaspoon salt
2 cups hot water
7 cups milk, added 1 cup at a time
2 teaspoons vanilla

In slow cooker combine first 5 ingredients. Blend in the hot water, mixing well. Turn slow cooker on low setting and continue heating the mixture until hot, but not boiling. Add milk, stirring after each cup is added. Let the hot cocoa blend for 2-3 hours before serving. When you are ready to serve, remove the cinnamon sticks and add the vanilla. With an electric mixer, beat the cocoa on low speed to form a frothy, foamy top. Serve immediately.

Excerpted from Crazy About Crockery! 101 Recipes for Entertaining at Less than .75 cents a serving ISBN 1891400525 by Penny E. Stone

Hot CranApple Punch

8+ servings

1 gallon Cranapple® drink
46 ounces apple juice
46 ounces Hi-C Apple® drink
10 (2-3 inch) cinnamon sticks, tied in cheesecloth
20 whole cloves, tied in the cheesecloth
2/3 cup brown sugar

Combine all ingredients in a large slow cooker and turn on low setting. Simmer for a minimum of 3 hours. Remove the cheesecloth packet and stir the punch before serving.

Excerpted from Crazy About Crockery! 101 Recipes for Entertaining at Less than .75 cents a serving ISBN 1891400525 by Penny E. Stone

Mistletoe Punch

8+ servings

10 cups cranberry juice cocktail
5 cups orange juice
4 cups water
1 1/3 cups sugar
6 cinnamon sticks, broken into pieces
3 whole oranges, peeled and cut into wedges
1/2 teaspoon nutmeg
8 teaspoons instant tea powder
Skewered whole fresh cranberries

Combine cranberry juice, orange juice, water, sugar, cinnamon, nutmeg and orange wedges in slow cooker. Turn on high setting and bring to a boil. Stir in tea when mixture is boiling hot. Add the skewered cranberries. Reduce heat setting to low and keep the punch warm, blending and mellowing the flavors. Serve as desired, either warm from the slow cooker, or chilled over ice.

Excerpted from Crazy About Crockery! 101 Recipes for Entertaining at Less than .75 cents a serving ISBN 1891400525 by Penny E. Stone

Tanya's Hot Wassail

Serves many

1 gallon apple cider

2 large cans frozen grape juice concentrate

4 (grape juice) cans of water

8 tablespoons brown sugar

4 cinnamon sticks

1 teaspoon allspice

15 whole cloves

Bring to a simmer in a large slow cooker and serve warm, right out of the pot.

Excerpted from Cooking for Blondes: gourmet recipes for the culinarily challenged ISBN1891400940 by Rhonda Levitch

Andy's Mulled Cider

8-10 servings

1 (46 ounce) jug sweet apple cider
Several cinnamon sticks
Several whole cloves
1 cup brandy or rum (optional)
1 can of 7-Up® (optional)

Combine all ingredients in slow cooker and bring to boil on high setting. Turn setting to low and let flavors "mull" for 2 hours. Serve warm

Cook's Note: Brandy or Rum can be added into individual mugs at time of serving, if you elect not to mull it in the punch.

—from the kitchen of the Rush Hour Cook's Husband, J. Andrew Stowers

Dipped Jellied Candies

White chocolate, broken into chunks
Large gum drops or jellied candy slices
Tooth picks
Kids (under supervision)
Waxed paper

Gently melt white chocolate in the slow cooker, stirring constantly. Using toothpicks spear the candy and submerge into the melted white chocolate to coat. Transfer to waxed paper and let coating cool. Remove tooth picks and store in airtight container.

—from the kitchen of Robin Sabatke

About the Author

A Wisconsin resident, Wendy Louise currently lives near her Daughter, Son-in-Law and Granddaughter. When she is not busy pursuing life long interests in the fine arts, quilting, crafting and gardening she turns her interest to cooking and sharing in the family dinner hour. She believes that enjoying good food is one of the finer pleasures in life and that eating well is an important element toward family comfort and well-being.

RECIPE INDEX

INDEX
(for *Tips from the Kitchen...*)

Chapter Indexes:

This book includes many wonderful recipes that have been excerpted or adapted from the following Champion Press Ltd. Books:

by Brook Noel a.k.a. The Rush Hour Cook
JOIN THE FREE DAILY RUSH CLUB www.rushhourcook.com
The Rush Hour Cook: Family Favorites $5.95
The Rush Hour Cook: One-Pot Wonders $5.95
The Rush Hour Cook: Effortless Entertaining $5.95
The Rush Hour Cook: Presto Pasta $5.95
The Rush Hour Cook: Weekly Wonders $16

by Deborah Taylor-Hough
Frozen Assets: Cook for a Day, Eat for a Month $14.95
Frozen Assets Lite & Easy: Cook for a Day, Eat for a Month $14.95
Frozen Assets Readers' Favorites $25.00
Mix and Match Recipes: Creative Recipes for Busy Kitchens $9.95

By Rhonda Levitch
Cooking for Blondes: gourmet recipes for the culinarily challenged by Rhonda Levtich $27.95/hardcover $16/paperback

By Penny E. Stone
365 Quick, Easy and Inexpensive Dinner Menus (Over 1000 recipes!) $19.95
Crazy About Crockery: 101 Easy & Inexpensive Recipes for Less than .75 cents a serving $12.00
Crazy About Crockery: 101 Soups & Stews for Less than .75 cents a serving $12.00
Crazy About Crockery: 101 Recipes for Entertaining at Less than .75 cents a serving $12.00

By Leanne Ely
The Frantic Family Cookbook: mostly healthy meals in minutes $29.95 hardcover, $14.95 paperback
Healthy Foods: an irreverent guide to understanding nutrition and feeding your family well $19.95

TO ORDER
Read excerpts, sample recipes, order books and more at www.championpress.com
or send a check payable to Champion Press, Ltd. to 4308 Blueberry Road, Fredonia, WI 53021. Please include $3.95 shipping & handling for the first item and $1 for each additional item. Wisconsin residents please add .056 % sales tax.